Congratulations!
YOU'RE A
MILLIONAIRE!

*The Secrets to
Selling Your Way
to a Fortune*

B·R·I·A·N · G·O·T·T·A

FOREWORD BY CABELL BRAND
Co-Founder of the Direct Selling Association

Congratulations!
You're A Millionaire!

Brian Gotta

Copyright©2001 by Brian Gotta
Website: www.booksbygotta.com
e-mail: brian@booksbygotta.com

ISBN 0-938716-11-5

Published by
Possibility Press
Markowski International Publishers
One Oakglade Circle, Hummelstown, PA 17036
Phone: (717) 566-0468; fax: (717) 566-6423
Voice Mail: (717) 558-1780
e-mail: posspress@aol.com
Website: www.possibilitypress.com.

Cover photo: Digital Imagery© copyright 2001 PhotoDisc, Inc.

Manufactured in the United States of America

* * *

Dedication

This book is dedicated to my brother Kurt, who taught me to compete and never quit; to my father-in-law Dave, whose entrepreneurship inspired me; and mostly to my wife Kris, the smartest person I know, for giving me the confidence and reason to write this book.

Contents

—$—

Foreword

You may have read many books on salesmanship, but you will never read one with more practical down-to-earth advice and "how-to" than Brian Gotta's book, *Congratulations! You're A Millionaire!* In fact, the publisher, Possibility Press, has specialized in "how-to" books from *No Excuse!* to *Get A GRIP On Your Dream, SOAR to the Top, Reject Me—I Love It!, Brighten Your Day With Self-Esteem,* and many others.

Brian Gotta continues with these themes, but with specifics on how to capture your dream—how you can earn it—how, indeed, *you can become a millionaire.*

As Brian points out, everyone wants to be a millionaire. Even the popular television show and the increasing number of people who gamble or play the lottery, show that everyone wants to strike it rich. Brian teaches you how to do it, step by step, day by day, year by year.

This is not a theory book. It is a book of fundamentals, written by someone who has done it all his life.

Even though I, too, have been a salesman and have been in the selling business all my life, I still learned from Brian's book! I learned again the fundamentals of discipline, honesty, enthusiasm, self-confidence, and planning the use of your time. Basically, this book tells you how to get started and stick with it.

Brian points out that he started out in the vacuum cleaner business. But whether you are selling vacuum cleaners, windows, insurance, household environmental products, or something else—the principles are the same.

You need to set goals and be motivated. You also need to follow certain rules of presentation and how to get over the fear of making cold calls. Brian's book helps with all of this.

He compares selling to baseball. A baseball star is one who bats 300. That means he strikes out about two out of three times. But it's that one hit in three that keeps you going and makes you successful. When you make six presentations a day and close one in three, you will make two sales a day or 50 sales a month.

The principle of being a millionaire is really quite simple. If you are selling a product that can earn you $400 net on a sale and you make 50 sales a month, you'll earn $20,000 a month, or $250,000 a year. Just think what that could mean to you.

If you save half of this and live on $125,000 a year, in less than eight years you will have $1,000,000 in the bank and still be earning $250,000 a year. If you have $1,000,000 in the bank and just live on the investment income of 6 to 8 percent or even 10 percent, you can have $60,000 to $100,000 worth of income without touching your equity. That's called security.

All you need is a product you can have confidence in, coupled with a company that will back you up and help you get started. And the first step to getting started is to decide that this is the opportunity for you.

The opportunity is there. However, you need the desire, the discipline, and the motivation to take advantage of it. Brian shares with you how to do this, while helping you understand the basic issues of salesmanship. I can hardly wait for his second volume, which will give you more of the details of how to close a sale.

Other than my family, and the work I have done in the community, the thing that I am the most pleased about at my stage in life is the people our companies have helped to succeed and capture dreams bigger than they ever thought possible.

That is what this book is all about—the "how-to" of selling your way to your fortune. Now read this book and go for it! You really can.

Cabell Brand
**Co-Founder, Former Chairman, and
Hall of Fame Member of the
Direct Selling Association**

Introduction

——§——

The Dream and The Reality

*"Wealth is not attained by the small investment
that hits the jackpot, but rather by properly investing
in the two biggest assets you have:
your time and your desire."*
Brian Gotta

ongratulations! You're a Millionaire! Virtually every little boy and girl dreams that someday he or she will be a millionaire. How about you? To most people, the thought of being a millionaire brings up lavish images. It means being *rich* and having no worries. We may think of attending private parties; "rubbing elbows" with the elite; having all the time in the world to do what we want to do—spending more time with our families, traveling, indulging in our hobbies, enjoying our sports—and having the finest homes, nicest cars, and *certainly* no money challenges!

Unfortunately, for most people these images seem so implausible—so farfetched—that it's no more than a fantasy to them. They think these things happen only to *other* people—the chosen few who live the lucky life most everyone else dreams about—but never attains.

This explains our fascination with movie stars, professional athletes, and tabloid journalism. It's as if by watching the rich and famous on stage, screen, the playing field, or in their other arenas we can somehow live vicariously through their talents and efforts. We may ultimately make them heroes—only wishing we could be like them.

Similarly, such dreaming offers an explanation for the popularity of lotteries, gambling casinos, and the perpetual "get rich quick" schemes we always hear about. We are all drawn to the idea of a small investment which, when mixed with a lot of luck, will hit it big for us and solve all our financial problems. "If *only*...," we may comment, not really believing we could do it too.

Okay, let's get back to reality.

Do you *really* think the big, lucky strike will happen for you? Did you ever wonder why the gambling industry is constantly building new and larger casinos with more garish adornments? Or have you ever considered why, state-run lotteries are more popular than ever?

The problem is, the odds of your winning anything substantial in any of these games of chance is pitifully small—so *not* in your favor. But the general public's desire to gain wealth without effort is so strong that the industry is growing like crazy, and somebody's getting rich alright, but it's not you!

So you'd like to be a millionaire too. Who wouldn't? They even named one of the most popular U.S. game shows in history *Who Wants to be a Millionaire?*

Who wouldn't like to be more in control of their life and their time? Who wouldn't like to be able to do whatever they wanted, whenever they wanted to do it? And of course, everyone would love to have the financial freedom to send their children or grandchildren to the best schools, drive the nicest cars, and enjoy the finer things in life.

But did you know you could become a millionaire, and it doesn't depend one iota on luck? And did you also know, as someone once said, "Luck is when opportunity and preparedness meet"? Wealth is not attained by the small investment that hits the jackpot, but rather by properly investing the two biggest assets you have: your time and your desire. In fact, you *can* surpass your greatest expectations and become what you have always dreamed of being—a millionaire!

That's where this book comes in. You will soon realize there are riches waiting right under your nose—all you need to do is claim them! This book is here to help you gain the tools you need to live a lifestyle basically only accessible to those who deserve it because they worked for it. (Very few millionaires inherited or won their wealth through a game of chance.)

This book features formulas you can use to succeed in the business world, as well as motivating ideas that can help spur you into action. You'll find practical ways to attain what for most people is a lifelong ambition, sadly unrealized. It will teach you how to sell, work, and win.

In short, when you heed and put into deed what you read, you *will* succeed!

Chapter One

—$—

Could This Be for You?

*"Destiny is not a matter of chance,
it is a matter of choice; it is not a thing to be
waited for, it is a thing to be achieved."*
William Jennings Bryan

What is a millionaire? Being referred to as a millionaire used to mean an individual had earned more than one million dollars in his or her career or business. More people today use the term to apply to someone with a million dollars in liquid assets. However you choose to define it, most millionaires do not necessarily live a glamorous, movie star life. Most are just like the majority of people—they have families and ordinary lifestyles—by choice.

The reward for earning a substantial income does not have to be glamorous to be appealing. It could mean private schooling for your children or that your spouse could stay home with your children instead of sending them to day care. Perhaps it would mean owning a home free and clear of debt, having a nice car paid for, and possibly even a boat or airplane—bought with cash.

You may imagine that the greatest benefit to earning a comfortable living is not having to stop and consider the budget every time you want to make even a relatively small purchase. And maybe you could even quit work before you are 65 and retire with more income from your investments than you had while you were working. Wouldn't nearly everyone love to have all of the above and more? Ironically, these rewards are *available to all*, but they are claimed by just a few.

Who Can Be a Millionaire?

In our society, there are four categories of people who earn well above average incomes, and they all have something in common: They earned their income based strictly on results. First, there are professional athletes and entertainers, and they get paid to perform. Next there are doctors, lawyers, and other professionals who are paid when they assist patients or clients. The third category consists of conventional or franchised business owners. They risk some or all of their own money, and they get paid for attracting and serving clients or customers.

Finally you have people who are in direct sales or sales management. These individuals may work as reps for a corporation. Or, they may be independent business owners who often work from home and may be financially linked to an organization of other independent business owners who use the same supplier. They may pay a small price to get started, including some products and maybe some tools like tapes and books/manuals. As with the first three, this fourth category is paid for results as well.

Can It Happen to You?

If you seriously want to be highly paid—if being a millionaire is not just a fantasy for you—what are your options? Do you expect to be drafted soon by a professional sports team and sign a million-dollar contract? Or do you have some rare talent in the entertainment field that could earn you a high income? If not, do you have the time or the resources to go to law or medical school?

Do you have the money to start up your own conventional or franchised business? And if you did, would you risk it, knowing that 80 percent of all new businesses fail each year, many due to under capitalization?

If your answer to all of the above questions is no, what are you left with? A career or business in direct sales—a profession where you are paid based on your performance. And depending on the structure of the business and where you are positioned, you may have others you manage or bring into your business as associates.

Taking Responsibility

Like anything else worthwhile, making the decision to get involved with sales of any kind requires courage. However, you've made the right choice if you like the idea of being in control of your schedule, your income, your advancement, and your future. Nowhere is there a better opportunity for you to control your own destiny, and perhaps help others do so as well. When you honestly examine your potential in this arena, it can be very exciting. It gives you a real chance to learn, grow, and prosper.

Control is a word you will read again and again, because in sales you have a great deal of control of virtually everything relating to your career or business. This, of course, can vary, depending on the organization or corporate supplier you're tied into. But generally speaking, you have considerably more autonomy in sales. When asked, most people say this is a great thing—they definitely would like to be in command of their future.

However, there is a trade-off to gaining this control that people in sales need to accept. Most people would have to give up something they have become very familiar and comfortable with—the treacherous pattern of making excuses and laying blame for every problem or pitfall they ever create or encounter.

Often, people who are not happy with their lot in life blame others for their misery. They find it easier to blame their jobs (that *they* chose!) for not having enough time with their family, rather than taking responsibility by asking for what they want, changing jobs, or perhaps having their own business. It's easier for them to moan that the deck was stacked against them, and that's why they haven't achieved their financial goals. By blaming someone or something else, without even knowing it they give away their power to make a positive and often necessary change.

The fact is, the *real* reason they haven't saved for retirement, haven't been able to take the vacations their friends take, or haven't gotten ahead is *not* because of someone or something else. It's because of *them* and what they did or failed to do along the way.

The Mirror Never Lies

In sales, people can't honestly blame anyone but themselves for their failures. When they are evaluated and paid strictly on performance it is not the boss's fault, their employing company's fault, their leader's fault, their corporate supplier's fault, the government's fault, or anyone else's fault that they did not succeed. If any setbacks occur, no matter how uncomfortable or unusual it may be to do so, people need to look in the mirror to find the responsible party.

The great news is, however, that you also don't have to share any credit for your success because you're doing the work—whatever it takes to be successful in your industry—which may include leading others. You can arrive at any station in life you choose, confident in the knowledge that your success started with your initial desire to succeed. And you don't have to bow down to anyone or depend on luck or nepotism. (You may, however, wish to honor or acknowledge your mentor—the person who helped you develop your skills and who may have worked with you—at least to get you started.)

In sales, since results speak for themselves, you're paid and promoted or otherwise go to new levels strictly according to the monetary worth of the products or services you, and possibly your employees or associates sell.

By contrast, most people with ordinary jobs don't feel they're overpaid, or for that matter, even paid what they deserve. Unfortunately, few people do anything about their situation. They just "settle for" what they consider their lot in life. They choose to complain and go through life without taking control—even to the point of not asking for what they want from their employer. They spend their lives working for someone other than themselves, being paid minimally, with most of the fruits of their labor profiting only their bosses or the corporation.

These people often see themselves as victims of a crime, when they are really accessories to it. Without their cooperation, their sad state of affairs wouldn't exist. The minute they have the courage to realize they *do* have a choice and do not *have* to willingly participate, they can step outside the mental box they've been in and assume control. Hopefully, at some point, this is what you have done for yourself and your family, and, if so, can feel good about having taken that first step. Since most people don't have the level of understanding to do so, you have already done something extraordinary.

The Most Important Investment You Can Make

The more your income is based solely on incentives (commissions and bonuses), the more unpredictable it can be. But ironically, a commission and bonus-based income also gives you considerably more potential for exceptional earnings and advancement to new positions or levels. When you compare the way you earn money to the way you invest it, you'll notice a parallel.

Imagine what would happen if you put some money in the safest form of investment available—a plain, government insured savings account at a local bank. There is no risk whatsoever of your investment diminishing, and you'll receive a small, simple interest rate guaranteed. This is like taking a job that pays a flat hourly wage or a salary. Playing it safe with the bank may seem like the most secure investment move you can make. However, the tiny interest rate the bank pays you for using your money won't even keep up with the inflation rate. And over time, that initial amount of capital will be worth less and less, making it a bad investment.

Put that same amount instead into something with more risk, such as stocks or mutual funds, and watch what happens over time. There may be some lean years where the stock market performs poorly, possibly even returning less than a simple savings account. But more often than not, there will be years where the market does so phenomenally well it more than makes up for the lean stretches. During the last fifty years overall, most long-term stock market investors have decidedly outperformed long-term investors in savings or money market accounts. This is what can happen when you're paid on *performance*.

This book is not to teach you how to invest your financial resources. Instead, it is designed to help you invest the greatest assets you possess—your *time and desire*.

Suppose you inherit a sizable amount of money today. It's not enough to retire on—but a large enough sum that, with careful investing, it could have a meaningful impact on your financial future. Wouldn't you do your best to put your nest egg where it could stay for a while, grow, compound, and accrue more than just simple interest?

The truth is, you *have* inherited a large sum of money, and it is in your head, your back, and your heart. That sum is called your *ability*, *potential*, *time,* and *desire*. You can foolishly waste it all little by little, diminishing its value through the years by never taking any risks. Or you can invest it wisely, take calculated risks, experience some highs and lows, and over your sales career or period of business ownership, watch it grow, flourish, and multiply as long as you don't quit.

Could the potential benefits of a sales career or business be worth some uncertainty along the line? Sure! Besides which, your life can become a more vibrant experience in the process—full of hope and anticipation. That, to many who have chosen sales as their path to success, is a reward in and of itself. No more "same old, same old"!

How Secure Is a Salary, Really?

All too often, when people are job hunting they are looking for the so-called safety blanket of their next position. Again, too many people have the mistaken notion that a salary is more secure than a commission. In reality, *a salary is only secure as long as someone chooses to pay it.* As soon as the company downsizes or the boss's nephew or niece graduates from college, you may once again be looking in the help wanted ads.

Instead of thinking, "I need to get a $500-$600/week salary at my next job," you need to say to yourself, "How am I going to earn between $700,000-$1,000,000 in the next ten years?" You'll most likely be earning money somewhere, or in some way, ten years from now. But if between now and then you're only earning $500-$600 or even $700 per week, then it's highly likely you'll be no better off ten years from now than you are today. In fact, depending on the rate of inflation and other challenges you have along the line, you could even be worse off! You may be thinking you're not qualified to earn $700,000-$1,000,000 over the next ten years on any type of a salary. So what does that leave? Being paid on performance!

These days, it's rare to find a salaried employee who is not apprehensive about layoffs, downsizing, or pay cuts. In a commission sales job, though, when you're producing very well, it is logical that you're less likely to be eliminated. Agree? You're more likely to be viewed as an asset than a detriment to the "bottom line." In direct sales, as an independent business owner, representative, dealer, distributor, associate, or whatever you're called, you have the chance to build your own business without the fear of anyone eliminating your opportunity to provide income for yourself and your family. Yes, it's true there's more risk. However, these business people, who earn income strictly on their results, are free of those employee worries. Like commission-based sales employees, any revenue they bring in is purely *incremental,* a gain, to the company. Therefore, as long as it's ethically obtained, the company will always gladly accept these sales and reward the business owner accordingly.

Get Into Sales and Give Yourself a Raise!

By choosing a sales career or business you've chosen a lifestyle independent of most of the concerns associated with ordinary jobs. Don't like your boss? In sales you're either totally or pretty much your own boss. Tired of working harder for the same pay as others? Never again will *your* dedication subsidize someone else with less ambition and ability, who is content to do the bare minimum needed to receive a paycheck.

In sales, as long as you are associated with an ethical company, you are paid exactly what your results are worth—not a penny less. Your job or business will always be fresh as you progressively reinvent yourself while meeting and talking to many interesting people, and fine-tuning your skills and abilities.

Your day will be filled with ups and downs, triumphs and failures, and feelings of accomplishment that will help you feel a new, exciting vitality. Never again will you be a slave to a clock, bored by a monotonous routine-filled workday, or left without a sense of fulfillment. You'll never again feel the frustration of doing more than was necessary and having no one notice. Your success will reflect it.

You'll learn how to better communicate with people, what makes them "tick," and how to help them feel better about themselves. And you'll discover how to benefit them while benefiting yourself in the process. Each sale you make will help drive the economy of the country where you live, and add yet another layer to your self-confidence. When you have spent a year of dedication in sales you will have earned the equivalent of a degree in psychology and sociology, and you will have been paid well along the way for the education.

You're making the right choice when you invest your time and talent in an honorable sales career or business. And when you stick with it, the effort you put forth can pay you and your family huge dividends for life.

Chapter Two

—$—

Believe in the Law of Averages

"Keep going until you win.
After that, you'll want to go even more
and win bigger than before."
John Fuhrman

What's the secret to sales success? If you study the top producers in any sales company, you'll notice they all have one thing in common. Each of them speaks to huge volumes of people and makes many more presentations than those who don't succeed. They understand this is a numbers game, and the more people they talk to about their products, services, or opportunity, the more yeses they get, plain and simple. They realize that instead of talking to a very few people who they feel are definite yeses, if they instead get in front of a *lot* of people, regardless of any expressed interest, the law of averages works in their favor.

You may know or currently be associated with someone who is a tremendous salesperson. He or she may make it look easy, and seem to have been born with the knack. But how do you think "natural" salespeople got that way? Do you think that in their first ever presentation they were as good as they are now? No way! They got that way simply through steady practice, trial and error, and talking with so many people that they honed their skills as quickly as they possibly could.

In every sales business there is a quotient or ratio of presentations to sales that company veterans achieve. For "x" number of presentations done, you can realistically expect "y" number of yeses. When you're new and inexperienced, your ratio may not be quite as high as the ratio of someone who has been around a while, and that's understandable. A better average comes with practice, time, and experience— just like it does for a baseball player. Whatever the ratio might be in your industry, learn to concentrate your focus on the higher number, the one corresponding to the number of presentations you need to do to be successful.

Even though you get *paid* on the sales volume you bring in, your income is still going to be directly proportional to the number of presentations you make. As soon as you understand and work the numbers, much of the anxiety that often comes along with a new sales business or career decreases. As a result, the level of control you have in your ability to earn increases. As long as you do the presentations, and fine-tune your skills along the way, the yeses will follow.

There are several reasons why looking for presentations instead of looking for yeses is to your advantage. But the first is that doing so makes your job or business so much easier.

Don't Prejudge—Just Draw Your Cards

In business, you really cannot control who buys from you or decides to become associated with you. In fact, anyone in sales for any length of time will tell you there are some people who simply will not buy from or associate with you. And no matter how skilled you are, there is no way of knowing whether or not a prospect will buy or "get in" (in the case of sharing an opportunity) until you make your presentation.

At the same time, there are also a certain number of clients or customers or potential associates who *will* buy from or associate with you. And again, you won't know who they are until you do your presentations. Since you can't control which people are going to say yes and which are not, you'd better not wake up in the morning or come home from your regular "day job" or business and start looking for a yes, because you have no way of knowing where it, or they, will show up!

Instead, a better plan of action is to determine every day the number of calls you need to make. And then *no matter what* (barring a true emergency, of course), make that number of calls! This makes your job or business easier because it gives you a simple target to focus on. The knowledge that you have an attainable, controllable task at hand will help you drive yourself to complete the required number of calls. After that, if one or more yeses are in the picture too, all the better! But if not, when you quit for the day or evening you can rest assured that you honestly did what you could do and you won't be crippled by your concern for how much money you made or how many associates you brought on that day.

Let's say that with your company or business the average person gets a yes for every four presentations he or she makes. Then think of yourself as drawing from a deck of cards. Every club, heart, and spade you draw from the deck is a presentation where you professionally represented your product, service, or opportunity to the best of your ability but weren't able to get a yes. Every diamond, however, is a sale that puts money in your pocket or adds an associate or new recruit to your organization.

If this were the case, wouldn't you want to draw as many cards as possible from the deck? In fact, say someone offered to let you draw as many as you wanted, paying you or giving you a new recruit on every diamond. You'd be drawing cards in a frenzy, barely slowing down to notice which suit each one was, wouldn't you?

You'd know that as long as you draw fifty-two cards (the entire deck) there would be thirteen diamonds. Draw one hundred and four cards, and there'd be twenty-six diamonds, and so on. Would you get discouraged whenever you drew a club, heart, or spade? Of course not! You'd only be thinking that each one of those "off suits" meant you were one closer to what? A diamond!

But guess what? Someone *has* made you that offer. You're in a unique position where you can earn as much as you desire and draw as many diamonds as you wish for the rest of your life. As long as you diligently continue to work at it, improving your skills as you go along, and enduring some hearts, spades, and clubs, you *will* succeed in sales.

One thing that makes sales so much fun is that every time you shuffle the deck, the cards are aligned in a different order. Sometimes all the diamonds are at the beginning of the deck, so after a hot streak (when you possibly think you're *never* going to miss again!) you'll need to endure a long stretch of the other suits. Another time you'll need to go through what seems like an endless string of hearts, spades, and clubs to get to the deck's first diamond. And sometimes the cards draw out almost exactly in a one out of four ratio. But rest assured, for every deck of fifty-two, somewhere, in some order, are your thirteen diamonds. You just need to keep drawing until you find them.

All too often new people come into the sales arena and quickly become discouraged because they don't get a yes from the first few people they see. They fail to realize that every no gets them that much closer to a yes. Therefore, a lot of noes is a positive thing, not a negative one.

Let's put this into perspective. Suppose two people start with a company at the same time. One of them does five presentations and makes three sales, or brings three associates on, while the second one does twenty presentations but only sells or recruits two. The first person may appear to have a temporary advantage. But look both of them up two or three decks of cards from now. For the first person, the law of averages is going to catch up, and he or she is going to start drawing some hearts, spades, and clubs. The law of averages will catch up to the second individual too, and he or she will start drawing plenty of diamonds. It's simple—at the end of the month, the one who drew more cards will have earned more business.

There is one more reason why you'll want to work with the law of averages. Since you're basically tied to a certain ratio of presentations to yeses, (even as your skills and practice improve the ratio, you can never totally overcome it), the more presentations you make, the more yeses you get. Unfortunately, you can never really tell before you draw a card which suit is going to turn up; therefore, you are wise not to prejudge and start trying to sell *before* you've even made a presentation. That simply doesn't work!

When people start selling or recruiting without a presentation, they've begun short-cutting—trying to cheat. It's as if they are too lazy to draw a card legitimately, so they're peeking under the deck to see if part of the top card is showing, attempting to determine if it's even *worth* drawing. Some people want to sell their product, service, or opportunity over the phone to a prospect, when they simply need to be striving to make an appointment to make their presentation. Some people attempt to determine whether there is a high level of interest from the prospect when they need to just do the presentation.

When you're looking for sales or recruits instead of just a chance to share or show what you have, you end up disqualifying yourself out of presentations that could have ended with a favorable result. It doesn't work to rush the process.

Prequalify Less—Present More

When people fall into the trap of selling without a presentation, they ask a slew of preliminary questions, hoping the prospective customer, client, or associate will say, "You know, I'd really be interested in taking a look at what you're selling and I may want to buy!" Or, "The opportunity you have to offer sounds like it may be just what I've been hoping for!" It's wishful thinking that people will necessarily want what you're sharing because it may seem like it *could* be beneficial to them. In reality, you may get shut down before you ever begin, because prospects won't buy or join something they know virtually nothing about. Also, you may be acting pushy, which is a turnoff.

It's not that the prospects aren't necessarily interested; you just need to give them a chance to learn about what you're offering. Hoping that the prospects will express a desire for what you have to share with them even though you may not have enough desire to fully show it, will only lead to disappointment. It behooves you, as an aspiring millionaire, to jump into the arena with both feet. Just start doing lots of presentations and, if appropriate, teach others to do the same.

By focusing unwaveringly on only the number of presentations you need to do and not looking for yeses, you'll close deals or bring in new recruits who early on gave no indication of being potential yeses. You'll find yourself someday walking away with an order or a new associate, scratching your head in amazement, and wondering why, of all the great presentations you made, *that* was the one that turned out to be the winner.

Pushing Them Back

There's another school of thought about prequalifying people that is applicable to those sharing an opportunity. It is often called "pushing them back." Basically this is verbally taking the opportunity away from them. It could be saying, "I don't know if you'll qualify or not," "My schedule is tight, but I'll see if I can fit you in," or something else that indicates the opportunity is valuable and that there's some doubt that they have what it takes. People are more likely to want something if it seems like it may be unattainable. It's just human nature.

The One Who Hears No the Most Wins!

Understand the value of your numbers (the law of averages for your business) and you'll have peace of mind. For example, Fred sold copiers for many years and was quite successful. He had seen a lot of new, eager young men and women come into his company, as salespeople. They would work at it for awhile, but then leave the business discouraged.

When asked what was the single thing he most attributed their lack of success to, he said, "In our business you're just like a good hitter in baseball, one out of three. My percentage has always been that for every three decision makers I have had a chance to meet with, I'll make a sale. The thing that caused the most challenges for our new trainees was not that they couldn't get the one out of three but that, for some reason, they couldn't accept the two out of three they missed."

"They get discouraged because they're not used to failing more times than they succeed, and they don't understand this is part of the territory. It's also why the pay is so great."

Fred said something all salespeople need to heed. Look at any good hitter in baseball. The batting averages of the best ones to ever play are in the .330-.350 range, roughly one out of three. This means they fail twice as often as they succeed. Even hitters who only hit .250 are paid millions to fail three out of every four times they get up to bat! Now doesn't that help you put the noes into perspective?

When You Get Up Often, the Hits Will Come

Great hitters, like great salespeople, are keenly aware that their careers or businesses are a numbers game. They know that seeing the ball well, making solid contact, and being able to drive the ball are the important aspects of each time they're at bat. If they hit the ball hard but right at someone who makes a play to get them out, they don't throw the bat in frustration or get down on themselves. They know they hit the ball hard, which was their intent, and they know they can't control what happens after that.

When the successful baseball players start a new season, they're concerned with how many times they'll get up to bat that year, not how many hits they'll get. Super hitters know that as long as they stay healthy and get up six hundred times that season, they'll have roughly two hundred hits. Some days they might go three for four, and the next two games only go one for eight. But as long as they get enough chance to swing the bat, the hits will come naturally!

Your job then is to go out every day or evening and focus on two things. First, ask yourself "How many cards can I draw or how many at bats can I get?" (How many times can I make my presentation?) Then do whatever it takes to get that number. Second, when you get up to the plate, hit the ball hard. In other words, give your presentation with enthusiasm and passion.

The rest of what you read will be devoted to making sure you know how to get up to bat, and that when you are up, you're the best hitter in your league.

Chapter Three

—§—

Enthusiasm Makes the Difference

*"Enthusiasm is more
important than intelligence."*
Albert Einstein

Enthusiasm sells. If you've recently gotten into sales or your own business, you're probably excited about your potential. But if you're a veteran of sales and business, you might need to recreate that excitement because you may no longer get the same thrill from it as you did when you first started.

It's common for rookies to join a company and right away start selling like they've been shot out of a cannon. They may even outsell the established top producers their first few months, leading everyone to think they're the new, up and coming superstars in the business. But then, their volume suddenly plummets.

They often start doubting themselves and ask, "Was I just lucky before? Is this really for me?" Others experienced in the business may endeavor to help by analyzing the newcomer's techniques and presentation skills. The sales veterans may ask, "Are you forgetting this step? Did you remember to tell them about this feature or benefit?"

What if you find yourself in this kind of situation? You've probably encountered a "sophomore slump." Your sales may be lacking not because of *what* you are doing in front of a prospect, but rather *how* you are doing it.

Have You Lost Your Touch?

The challenge may be that you no longer possess the same genuine enthusiasm you used to have. When you started in the business, you probably knew relatively little about the product, service, or opportunity. But you may have compensated by working hard and making such an enthusiastic presentation that your excitement was contagious.

It's likely prospects often wanted to be a part of what you had to offer because you were so fired up. Consequently, even though your presentation may have been lacking in technique and factual information, you may still have written many orders or brought several new associates on board— just because you were excited. It was obvious you were having fun and were eager to share what you had discovered with others.

To most of your prospects, you may have been irresistible. However, after a while the newness wore off for you and what you were doing became less fun and more of a chore. Your presentation may have become just rote-habit. Soon you and your approach may have become no different than that of any other average salesperson you were competing with.

Even though you had gained volumes of knowledge through experience, you may have imparted it to your prospects boringly. If only you could get back your original fervor for sales and combine it with your increasing sales savvy, you know you would be unstoppable.

If it's natural for some of the luster to wear off of any new position or business with time, how do you keep it fresh? How do you regain your enthusiasm and stay excited and motivated? How do you avoid falling into the trap of being boring when the "thrill of the hunt" is no longer as stimulating as it was in the beginning?

"Break a Leg"

Compare yourself in your sales career or business to an actor or actress in a long-running Broadway show and you may learn a lesson in professionalism. When the show was ready to run on opening night, you can bet the cast was a mixture of excitement, nervous energy and anticipation before the curtain rose for the premiere. The thrill they felt and the adrenaline surging through their veins lifted them to emotional heights they had never imagined. When that first performance was over, they wanted to recapture that euphoric, on-the-edge feeling again and again.

However, after performing the same show night in and night out for months, the cast may no longer feel the same enthusiasm they once did. In fact, they probably often feel the same way you may feel before going into work, perhaps wishing you could be doing something new and exciting. They may even think, "Here I go again, doing the same thing I did yesterday and the day before."

But the actors and actresses realize that for the audience, with rare exception, this is their *first and only* time to see the show. Their job then is to recreate the same excitement within themselves as they had that first night *every time* they go on stage. They need to see to it that no one sitting in the theater can tell the difference between this show and opening night.

What happens next is amazing. Because the performers act with passion and unrelenting enthusiasm, within minutes it overtakes them and *becomes* them. Before long, they are no longer acting. That is why they are professionals. And that's also why they are paid very well for doing what few others can do.

You might be asking, "What does this have to do with sales?" Everything! A part of every successful salesperson is a paid actor or actress. The top-drawer salesperson can be laden with personal challenges, be having a week with few or no yeses, or simply be tired and ready to go home. But when the lights go on and that curtain rises on yet another presentation, he or she shakes off their lethargy, rises to the occasion, and gets ready to deliver a dynamic and memorable performance. Within minutes, that performance turns into genuine enthusiasm which becomes contagious. As Walter Chrysler once noted, "The real secret of success is enthusiasm. Yes, more than enthusiasm, I would say excitement. I like to see people get excited. When they get excited, they make a success of their lives."

Control Your Attitude and You Control Your Success

To maintain your professionalism, you need to condition yourself to have the proper attitude. After all, this *is* a people business no matter how high-tech it's become for some of us. Your success depends on how you interact with the prospects and clients, customers, or associates you talk to. Will they like you, trust you, and want to buy from or associate with you? If you're friendly, eager, enthusiastic, passionate, and just plain nice, then the answer is much more likely to be yes! Your chances are increased dramatically that they will! (Few people want to associate with or buy from someone who has a lackluster attitude.) Add a solid belief in your product, service, or opportunity and a polite, knowledgeable presentation, a caring attitude about them, and you can become quite compelling. But again, it all starts with the attitude you project.

Each prospect becomes a mirror of your behavior. Present your case boringly and they will bore you. You may leave the presentation saying, "I couldn't get a yes from him; he had no life; he was a dead fish." Or strive to sell contentiously by refuting each objection you hear as if you and your product, service, or opportunity were on trial and you'll leave without a yes and thinking, "What an angry lady she was; no one could have sold her anything or recruited her."

More than likely, you'll make more headway when you smile warmly at your client, customer, or prospect, make eye contact, get excited, be interested in them, and act lively. Laugh, bringing some levity to the presentation along with sharing the facts and figures they need to make an educated decision, and then watch the response you get. You can help even the most surly, angry clients, customers, and prospects turn into warm and attentive people when you treat them kindly—the way you would like to be treated yourself.

In a few cases, no matter what you endeavor to do you may find you can't win over a quarrelsome person. Simply move on and know there are plenty of nice people just waiting for someone with your attitude and product, service, or opportunity to come along. And feel even better about yourself knowing *you* don't have a challenge with your attitude; the poor person you just left does. Always remember that nothing and no one, not even someone who is belligerent, can ruin your attitude without your permission!

It All Starts With a Smile

Getting yourself in the right frame of mind to sell or present enthusiastically begins with something very simple—a smile. A psychologist in San Francisco once did a study on the effects of smiling. The results were quite interesting. Incidentally, he also used professional actors, but in a different manner. This doctor performed a series of tests, showing photographs and asking questions designed to cause emotional stress in his subjects. As these people were tested, he carefully noted their physiological responses. The first time they went through the experiment with no specific instructions. Then the doctor asked all of them to participate in the same tests—while forcing themselves to smile.

The results? Even though the actors weren't smiling out of any real happiness—they were *just acting*—each of them came through the tests with less evidence of stress, simply by making themselves smile. The doctor concluded that simply by smiling, chemicals are released in the body which convince our brains that we are under less stress and are, in fact, more happy! So when you smile, even if at first it's contrived, you'll actually feel better and you're likely to create a smiling prospect. And everyone in sales will tell you they'd love to have a million of those.

Look at the World through Rose-Colored Glasses

There are many other ways to control your attitude and keep yourself in a positive frame of mind. For example, make sure you only dwell on the good things that have happened to you in your career or business, never on the challenges. In between calls, reminisce about the last sale you made or person you brought on. Relive the same emotions you felt the last time a customer said yes to you.

Occasionally give yourself certain little incentives, such as, "If I make "x" number of calls today by 5 p.m. (or this evening by 7 p.m.), I'm going to take my spouse out for dinner at our favorite restaurant." Make it a number you have to stretch for. Then, all day or evening long, until your "deadline," you'll have a short-term goal you're working for. If you don't make your goal, don't cheat! You're eating at home tonight. But when you do achieve your goal, reward yourself with a nice dinner out.

Read motivational personal development books, listen to uplifting motivational, educational tapes, attend enriching, enlivening seminars, and associate with the positive, successful people in your company or organization. Constantly fill your mind with the forward-thinking, inspirational words you need to maintain your optimistic outlook. Do it. It works!

Turn Negatives into Positives

For anyone thinking about a career or business in sales, enthusiasm is a necessity. And even if it's not the number one most important component to your presentation, it is definitely near the top. Your attitude is vital to your performance because it's what carries you through each day, week, month, and year as you encounter and rise above the challenges inherent to sales and success in general.

If you're new, the first thing you'll learn is that sales is an invigorating business—full of obstacles to overcome as you strive to be a peak performer. For every yes you get that puts money in your pocket or an associate in your organization, you'll need to endure many more noes—some courteous and some downright rude ones. You'll learn that at times you may do some of the most challenging personal growth inducing work you've ever done, and be sharper mentally than you've ever been *even though you won't get paid for it*—yet. But hang in there.

Sales requires a flexible, resilient, positive, can-do, never quit attitude. It requires looking at the big picture, not just the noes along the way. You need an entrepreneurial spirit, knowing that with continued persistence, you'll get to the yeses and the financial rewards will follow.

With the proper overall attitude, however, selling *is* fun. It can be the most enjoyable and lucrative vocation you could have ever imagined for yourself. More importantly, with strong enthusiasm and desire you'll learn quickly the most valuable thing a sales career or business can teach you. This is a life lesson that reaches well beyond the career or business you're in and makes an impact on your other day-to-day activities as well. It is something very few people know, yet it makes the biggest difference in every aspect of your life. The lesson that will ensure your productiveness and success in life is that with the right attitude, *you can turn every negative you ever encounter into a positive!*

For instance, what if you get discouraged because you haven't made a sale or gotten someone to sign up in a while, and you're working harder than a lot of people with average, salaried jobs? To the untrained person, that appears to be a negative. But the positive you see is that those people don't have the time freedom you have, and when you do get a yes or enough yeses, you might earn more in one hour than they do all week, all month, or maybe even all year!

Another example may come if you lose a sale or new recruit you thought you had. If you watch something you've worked so hard for slip through your fingers, and you let your attitude flounder, it can be disheartening. Many people would feel sorry for themselves and give up. But you'll realize this setback happened for a positive reason—you learned what you could have done differently so you can avoid making the same mistake next time. Now you've been strengthened by adversity, and this valuable lesson will put a thousand times more money in your pocket than you may have lost on just this one no.

When you teach yourself to possess this one skill, of looking at the bright side of difficulties, you have virtually conquered the world. Most successful people in sales have developed this ability. Since in sales the daily challenges can sometimes outnumber the positives a hundred to one, turning every one of those defeats into a victory will give you a strength of will no one can match. This is an attitude you could never master just by going to school and studying. It requires consistent practice in the real world. And if it *could* be handed out in the form of a diploma, that piece of parchment would be worth millions of dollars to anyone deemed worthy to receive it.

It's a Heavy Price, but It Brings an Even Greater Reward

In case you haven't realized it yet, a sales career or business is not for everyone. All people don't have a strong enough desire to develop the will to endure a hundred negative responses in order to gain one positive. Not everyone has a determination so potent, so burning within, to succeed and forge a better financial future for themselves and their families that they are willing to take on a task more challenging than that offered by the vast majority of vocations. And not everyone has developed the tenacity to endure a profession or business so filled with peaks and valleys. A chart of the emotional range the salesperson experiences on a weekly basis would look like a roller coaster to them.

But similarly, not everyone thinks they would ever have a real chance to become a millionaire, either. Not everyone honestly believes they will someday own their dream home, drive an expensive car, send their children or grandchildren to the best schools, live the lifestyle they yearn for, and retire early in comfort and style. Do you believe you and your family deserve these things? And with a point in the right direction and some guidance along the way, are *you* willing to pay the price required to achieve your dreams? If you are, then a sales career *is* for you.

And the enthusiasm and positive attitude you possess will be the vehicle that drives you toward your dreams.

Chapter Four

―――§―――

You Need Discipline and Desire to Make Things Happen

*"Put off what you want
to do for what you need to do."*
Brian Gotta

D o you need to develop more discipline and desire? There are two qualities, discipline and desire, that are extremely important to anyone who sincerely wants to succeed in sales and business. These two qualities are what separates the winners from the "also rans," and they are unfortunately lacking in more people than they are present. Without consistent discipline and true desire, most people find it difficult to attain a great level of success in sales, or in any other worthwhile endeavor.

Discipline is the ability to *habitually* make yourself do something you don't particularly want to do, even though you know it's good for you. Desire is the burning fire inside of you—the unwavering *want* for your passion and your goal.

Discipline and desire are not just words. They are the frame of your moral house—the blueprint of your future plans. Simply put, the most dominant aspects of your character are your discipline and desire levels. The two go hand-in-hand, one driving the other. If you lack discipline, it may be because you first lacked desire. Without desire, there is likely to be no discipline. Possess both and you can be an unstoppable force on your way to greatness.

It's Always *Your* Choice

If you look back on your life up to this point, each minute, hour, and day has been filled with choices. Every choice you've made so far has in some way contributed to the person you are today.

If you think back through all the choices you've ever made, it is likely you'll discover a common thread. You've undoubtedly been faced with the choice of taking either the easy path or the difficult one. The times you chose what appeared, in the short-term, to be the easy road resulted in ultimate long-term disappointment and dissatisfaction. But in the instances where you took the hard road, even though it was uncomfortable in the short-term, you gained the most long-term rewards.

Each day, as soon as the alarm clock goes off, you're faced with two choices. You can either do what would be easy—turn off the alarm and go back to sleep—or you can do the more difficult—get out of bed and go to work. We're able to exercise this discipline each morning because we know the consequences of the easy path would be so severe, (reprimands from a boss and eventually termination or failure of the business you may own), that we don't perceive it as a choice. It becomes one of the many things we've told ourselves we *have* to do.

The challenge is most of our choices are not that clear-cut. The majority of the daily forks in the road we face don't provide an immediate punishment for choosing the easy path. Since there are no easily apparent short-term consequences, we may actually be fooled into feeling *rewarded* for going the wrong way. Any guilt we may suffer we may easily push aside with procrastination, promising ourselves we'll make better choices tomorrow. As you may have experienced, it often seems easier to pick up a failure habit than it is to develop a success habit. It's all a matter of focus. You get what you focus on!

Focus on the results you're looking for and develop habits, as challenging as that may be, to support getting what you want. It all boils down to the choices you make day in and day out, large and small.

What Kind of Wall Do *You* Want to Build?

The impact of each of these many, often seemingly, little decisions we make, which work for or against our achieving our dreams and goals, is like building a brick wall. One or two bricks stacked on top of one another look harmless. But after a month of adding a new negative-habit brick each day, the wall is waist high. A few months later it's eye level. After enough bricks have been laid, the wall is so tall we can't see what's on the other side.

If you make enough detrimental choices—opting for the easy way out instead of the more challenging—you build a wall between yourself and success. This wall may eventually seem so insurmountable that you give up hope of ever being on the other side, perhaps blaming your age, poor luck, insufficient education, or current circumstances for what you don't have.

This behavior is not just limited to the business arena; it overlaps into people's multifaceted personal lives as well. For example, many people may not see the consequences today if they overeat or don't exercise. That extra plate of food may look good, taste good and immediately feel good, but if they choose that path enough times, in most cases they'll have a weight challenge. Then, by the time they realize they need to shed some pounds, they may be so heavy that the idea of being able to do so seems too difficult. Now the wall they've built is so high that they may resign themselves to carrying around the burden of extra pounds. Or they often do yo-yo dieting—losing and regaining the same weight over and over again—often gaining more. They don't exert the consistent discipline required to erase the consequences of the hundreds of small, failure choices they've made in the past.

However, when you lay a strong enough foundation of success habits through discipline, you'll eventually forget there ever was another choice. The first bricks you lay of the new positive habit might be the most challenging. But once you begin to see some height to the wall you've built with your success-habit bricks—which gives you some measurable fruit for your labor—you then work fast and furiously, adding as many of these success bricks as you can.

You'll fight to make sure no one or nothing ever threatens what is now the success-inducing fortress you've built for yourself. You'll have begun to shift from what may have been just barely surviving to happily thriving. You'll be reaping the rewards of a life of discipline, and even the thought of going back to the other side of your positive-habit wall ever again will seem unthinkable. Your many beneficial choices become unconscious habits, and soon these habits become your new lifestyle.

A Little Pain Is Good for You

The majority of people act out of avoidance of pain and in pursuit of pleasure or reward. But this is dangerous, because what feels good now may hurt later. You need to remember that in sales there is a simple formula to follow that will guide you down the right path: *In the pursuit of your goals and dreams, short-term pleasure can lead to long-term pain, and short-term pain can lead to long-term pleasure.*

In many other jobs or businesses, your day is not so filled with choices as it is in sales. In a salaried or hourly wage paying, clock-in-clock-out type position, after you make that initial decision to drag yourself out of bed and into the office or workplace, you may have to make one more meaningful choice all day: either stay and work until quitting time or re-sign. But quitting without enough income or resources to support ourselves won't lead to a pleasant experience. So all too often we stay in what we consider to be a dead-end, low-reward job, complaining the whole way and feeling trapped. Yet all the while, we are free to take any other path we choose. We have trapped ourselves mentally with yet another failure habit and gotten ourselves into an ungratifying, per-haps boring, "rut."

On the other hand, you need to use the tremendous free-dom that often comes with sales as wisely as possible. When you can become the focused master of yourself to choose and manage your activities well, both financially and timewise, you can go on to prosper from your excellent ability to virtu-ally or really be your own boss and set your own schedule. You can go see your son or daughter's sports activity or school program without needing to ask permission from any-one or having your performance suffer. You can generate more income than most people while working fewer hours, or earn extraordinary income by working more hours!

To appropriately use this time and money freedom re-quires you to make hundreds of success choices every day. Your supervisor, mentor, or leader probably doesn't have the time to follow you around on an hourly basis to make sure you're making the excellent choices necessary to be on target and be truly successful. You need to constantly manage your-self and make yourself work, even though there's no boss looking over your shoulder. This is why sales is either the easiest low-paying job in the world, or one of the most chal-lenging high-paying jobs.

Put Off What You Want to Do for What You Need to Do

Somebody once said, "*Maturity is delaying pleasure*." However, your maturity is not defined by the number of years you've lived—it's defined by your actions! An immature child acts strictly on impulses—immediate versus delayed gratification—doing only what feels good at the moment. Some parents strive to teach their children that by not instantly gratifying themselves, and by acting through intelligence rather than impulse, they will gain greater rewards and discover more freedoms. Parents who have not learned this lesson themselves, of course, cannot teach their children effectively!

When salespeople are out of the confines of an office on a regular basis, whether they are in a sales job or have their own full- or part-time business, they can be just like children. They can at anytime choose the immediate gratification of quitting early for the day or evening, thus making fewer calls than they know they need to. Later they may justify it—blaming their failures on almost anything, rather than admitting that they regularly exercise their success-defeating habit of procrastination. Each time they do this, they become more and more entrenched in their success-stealing habit; the wall gets higher and higher until they finally have the world's easiest *nonpaying* job or business.

Successful individuals keep themselves, as challenging as it may be, in the habit of doing the things the undisciplined refuse to do—and they don't procrastinate. Instead, they develop the habit of *delaying pleasure* which requires mature self-discipline. Resist the temptation to sneak off when nobody is looking. Put your head down and take the actions you know you need to take. Do this consistently over a long enough period of time and you'll be rewarded. You will earn the respect of your peers, the company you're associated with and, best of all, from yourself.

As a result of your persistent, unrelenting discipline, you'll acquire the freedoms everyone desires, as long as you keep going and growing—developing your skills and deepening your understanding of people and your industry along the way. You can make your dreams and goals a reality when you simply choose to invite discipline into your life and build a wall of success. Mark Twain once said, "Do something every day that you don't want to do. This is the golden rule of doing your duty without pain." Day by day, do your best to keep moving incrementally toward your goal of being a millionaire and living the life you want.

Your task, while not necessarily easy, is extremely simple: Just determine how many calls and presentations you need to make on a daily basis to provide the income you desire. Then every day, no matter what, do that number of calls and presentations. When you accomplish this, over a sufficient period of time, you will accomplish your financial goal.

Only through discipline will you achieve riches. With those riches you can own your dream home free and clear of debt, and give your children the finest education you can afford by paying cash. You'll also have more time to spend with your family, travel as much as you want, have more time and money to indulge in your favorite recreational activities, have a worry-free retirement, and do many other things that come along with having a great income.

But the question is, "How much do you really *want* those things?" This isn't asking, "Do you *wish* for them?," "Would you *like* to have them?," or "Would you *take them if* they were *given* to you?" Everyone knows the answer to those questions. And everyone would live the good life if there were no cost involved to get it.

But there is a cost, as in doing anything else worthwhile. So, again, the question is, "How much do you really *want* those things?" Are you serious about it?

Are You Willing to Pay the Price?

This is where desire comes into play. Because most people in developed countries have what they *need*, the question to ask yourself is, "Do I have what I *want*?" Having what you need means you're going to be able to put food on the table tonight. Even if you are suffering through tough financial times, you're still able to keep a roof over your head. People almost always maintain the bare necessities—just what they need to survive, and no more.

The real question is, "Do you have what you really, truly *want*?" If not, then why not? If it's because you believe you haven't yet been given the opportunity, you're in luck. This book will teach you how to seize the opportunity in front of you, wrestle it to the ground victoriously, and then get up looking for another challenge.

Perhaps you've had the opportunity—maybe even more than once—yet you *still* may not have accomplished what you have been saying you want because of a lack of desire or discipline. You may have decided to settle for what you already have, even though you're bored and unhappy, because you weren't motivated enough to take action.

So what can you do today to start making other choices? You need to decide right here and now what exactly it is you want out of your life. Is a life of disappointment, mediocrity, unfulfilled dreams, and losing lottery tickets *really* what you want? If not, can you get up, starting today and then every day from now on, and discipline yourself to do something about it?

Of course you can! The price you may have to pay, though, is a steep one. You may at times wonder if it's all worth it. Be assured—*it is!* Once you reach your goal, you'll look back and say, "This is definitely worth all the work it took to get here." Then you'll set yourself another goal and reach it too, while gaining so much more confidence! You'll be in an "upward spiral" instead of a downward one.

When you take that burning desire and, like a blacksmith, forge it with discipline, every day hammering it into a bright, extraordinary life for you and your family, you'll wonder how you ever dwelled on the other side of that huge wall of failure habits. You'll feel really good about yourself for having taken on one of the biggest and most rewarding challenges of your life—and emerging a winner! And to top it off, the great news is, along the way you'll make more true friends, who are also stretching toward their goals and dreams, and you'll have a lot of fun too!

Get Up and Go!

Now is the time to act. Kiss procrastination goodbye—it can be one of your worst enemies. Unsuccessful salespeople delay the inevitable; they essentially waste more time than they make good use of by not forcing themselves into action. You may be enthusiastic and educated, but unless you *do* something with it, that enthusiasm and education won't do you much good.

Get up and get yourself in front of prospects NOW! No one ever made any money in sales by sitting around just doing maintenance paperwork or reorganizing their contact list for the tenth time—being busy, rather than productive. But you can always find plenty of people around who do that and then, when they don't reach their goals (if they have even set any!), blame others or their circumstances for their lack of success!

It may be a challenge to find somebody who "rolls up their sleeves" and gets out with you and works—who does whatever it takes. But it's not coincidental that you'll easily find plenty of people leading financially unrewarding lives who aren't millionaires.

Be a great example—show others what they need to do by doing it yourself. Get out of the quicksand of the unmotivated and get your day or evening started! It's this simple: If you get off to a late start in the morning (or in the evening, if you're endeavoring to build a strong secondary income), your productivity will suffer. You know how many calls and presentations you need to make each day. Strive to have forty to fifty percent of those calls and presentations done before lunch or a designated time in the evening, say 7 p.m. Imagine how successful you will be when you follow this formula every working day!

You are not paid by the number of hours you spend away from home or your employer's office building, but rather by the *quantity* of clients, customers, or prospects you get in front of. So why wouldn't you want to get going early, make the required number of calls and presentations and be done with it? The quicker you do what you need to do for the day the sooner you'll be free to do what you want to do! But unfortunately, as you may have discovered, it is easier to procrastinate than to make that first call. Those that win in the game of sales, and in life, for that matter, break their inertia and *get moving*.

Get in the Water or Run Through the Woods

You may remember a hot day when you were at the beach or the pool. As you lay there baking in the sun, you began to get uncomfortably warm and wanted to cool off. But looking at the water, you knew it would be ice cold. So you found yourself in a dilemma.

You knew getting in the water was what you really needed to do, but you weren't anxious to get hit by that initial brace of cold. So you continued lying there and putting it off. Finally, when you just got *too* hot, you got up and approached the water. But then what happened? Did you first put one toe in the water until it was used to the temperature, then your whole foot, then the other foot—slowly and agonizingly wading in one body part at a time?

No, it's likely you took a deep breath and dove right in, so that your discomfort was minimized to split seconds, not minutes. Then, within a short period of time, you were accustomed to the water temperature. In fact, it felt good; and after swimming around, you were glad you braved that initial discomfort. Every day, at your first opportunity, you need to get up out of that comfortable beach chair that is your home, office, or car, and without delay, jump in the water!

In sales, your day, your week, and your career or business are all analogous to walking through a dense forest in search of a clearing. The forest you go through represents the effort; the clearing is the reward. Every day you know what the task at hand is—you know how many calls and presentations you need to make. Before you begin that day's or evening's sales responsibilities, you're in front of the forest. The clearing behind it is there for you when you finish doing whatever is necessary that day. Then tomorrow you'll move ahead to the next forest, and when done with it, you'll find the next clearing.

That forest may look as if there are many challenges to overcome. It may not look like it's going to be easy to get through it from where you stand. So some people will see if maybe they can walk *around* the forest—thus avoiding the hurdles within it. They'll take a day or two to walk east, looking for a shortcut or an end to the forest somewhere. When they don't find an easier path, they walk back to their starting point and then walk west, searching in vain for a smooth trail or a break in the trees.

When they still don't find a shortcut around the challenges the forest represents, they convince themselves that they didn't walk far enough east the first time. So they make a week long trek in that direction. When that proves fruitless, they endeavor to do the same thing in the other direction. They may eventually get so frustrated in their attempts to circumvent the success process that they finally start in through the trees. But after they get scraped by a thorn or twist an ankle, they hobble back out resigning themselves to finding an easier way tomorrow.

Then there are the other people—the successful ones. They don't bother looking for an easier way. They realize the shortest distance between two points is a straight line. And they're so consumed by their desire to reach the clearing that, as soon as the sun comes up, they're out there plowing through that day's woods.

They, like the first group, also suffer some scratches and bruises—they may get wet and sometimes cold—but they're undeterred and reach the clearing early. The next day they do the same thing. They keep on going, regardless of the obstacles. All the while the others are now way behind—still moving east and west—fruitlessly seeking an easy way around the inevitable hurdles they need to overcome to become successful.

After a month or so of this trailblazing, a remarkable thing begins to happen to the ones who forged ahead each day through the trees. The forests begin to get smaller and easier to move through, and paths begin to appear. These men and women begin to have more time to enjoy what has become a pleasant walk in the woods. The clearings they now reach are even larger and greener. Soon these people make so much progress that they can get to two or three clearings in one day. And they know it's just a matter of time before they reach the final meadow of financial security and freedom they've always dreamed of finding. They're very excited and happy because they can now see it up ahead—all within their reach.

In sales, the door to opportunity—the entrance to the forest—is wide open. But no one is going to carry you through the door—the spaces between the trees. You need to get up and walk, or better yet, *sprint* into and through your day's or evening's sales activities—the awaiting forest.

After you finish the rest of this book, come back and read this chapter again. Once you've acquired the skills to master sales, the only things you need to become wealthy are a burning desire to succeed and a strong self-discipline to take appropriate action.

Chapter Five

———$———

Honesty Is the Best Policy

*"Whenever you complete a task or
overcome a challenge honestly, you get
a wonderful feeling. If you do it insincerely,
dishonestly, and without integrity, you risk
losing everything you've accomplished."*
Jay Rifenbary

Congratulations! You have made a great choice by getting into sales. Now you're ready to sell with enthusiasm and live a life of self-discipline, all because you have the unwavering and burning desire to succeed. You are only one step away from being ready to learn how to better approach, present to, and then close (win) a client, customer, or prospective associate.

That one final yet most important component you need to have is honesty. As Thomas Jefferson once said, "Honesty is the first chapter in the book of wisdom." And the first chapter in your book of sales needs to be the same.

You've certainly heard the expression: "What goes around comes around." Nowhere is that more true than in sales. When you treat your clients, customers, or associates with respect, deal with them honestly, and make serving them a priority, you can have a long and prosperous career or business. Picture every day of self-discipline as a brick in your wall of security, and honesty as the mortar that cements the bricks together.

Have Integrity

Bob, a salesman of refrigeration supplies, learned the importance of honesty the hard way. "When I was brand new to the company, I had a good month going and had a chance to be the leading rep in my division. With only three days to go in the month, I found myself in front of a dream prospect. He was a nice older gentleman who owned a restaurant, and it looked like he was going to buy my deluxe package. He just resisted with the same stall tactics I had been overcoming all month.

"I was sure that by dropping to my next best package, which would more than adequately fit his needs and reduce his cost by $300, he'd buy on the spot. I didn't think he'd even notice the difference between the two systems. But instead of explaining the differences and making the second package attractive, I blew it. I told him that in order to earn his business today, I would give away my commission, which wasn't true, and he could have the equipment for the lower price.

"Up until that point we'd had a great rapport; he admired my enthusiasm and friendliness and wanted to help me out. But when he heard me offer to drop off my commission, he balked. He caught me by surprise and told me he *wanted* me to make money on the deal—he didn't want to buy if I wasn't making money! He wanted a good deal, but he also knew that I needed to earn some income, and he wasn't going to have me do all this work for nothing.

"I tried to backpedal as best I could by telling him I didn't mind because I was working hard to lead the division in sales for the month. I told him that since I would have him as a future customer I'd make out in the long-run. But the bottom line was, he was a sharp old fellow and he must have sensed something wasn't right. No matter what I said to him, he wouldn't go for it. He told me to come back in a couple of hours to see him after he discussed it with his business partner. I still thought I had the deal, so I went off for a long lunch and then came back two hours later.

"He called me into his office and asked me again what the price was. He wanted me to be clear about what he would be getting for that price, and I explained it to him. Then he told me that while I was gone he had called my main office and asked them some routine questions about the product warranty. They told him the warranty was different depending upon which system he purchased. When he asked the difference, they explained that one package was the new system the company had just come out with and had a better manufacturer's warranty. The other package was last year's system, which was essentially the same, but had a lesser warranty and sold for about three hundred dollars less. At this point I became flustered. I tried to make up another story to explain myself, but the gentleman cut me short.

"Very nicely, he then proceeded to tell me that he'd let me come back just so he could explain to me that I should always give clients the ability to make choices based on accurate information. He told me he wouldn't be placing an order, but that he wished me luck from here on out. What hurt more than losing the sale was the look of disappointment in his eyes. I finished second for the month in my division, of course, by just one sale!

"Since then I've always adhered to the belief that an honest loss is always preferable to a dishonest gain. But I really believe that losing that sale early in my career set the tone for the success I've had since then. I've made more money since he sent me away humbled than I would have if I'd gotten away with it."

Your integrity is essential. Bob's story illustrates the fact that if you don't treat your clients or customers and associates honestly, you will always come out behind. As Sophocles once said, "Rather fail with honor than succeed by fraud." By concealing some fact about the purchase or opportunity that clearly would cause the prospect to reconsider, thus putting him or her at a disadvantage because it's something only you know, you would be making a serious mistake.

What it all comes down to is having integrity, doing the right thing, coming from the highest moral standards and convictions, and being considerate of others' feelings. You need to treat others honestly and kindly, as you would want to be treated if you were in their situation.

But with all that said, remember why you're there. You want to give everyone you meet the chance to learn about your product, service, or opportunity.

There are approaches you will be taught in your sales career or business that are designed as inducements for your prospective clients, customers, or associates to buy or join your team. When you truly believe in your product, service, or opportunity, you need to share it with others. This means it's important for you to develop approaches that enable you to get it in front of as many prospects as possible.

First you need to honestly care about those you're striving to serve and think of how they'll gain as much as, if not more than, you will. Then both you and your new clients, customers, or associates can benefit from your compassion, hard work, and effort.

Chapter Six

—— $ ——

Professionalism and Self-Confidence Will Carry You Through

"Always do your best.
What you plant now, you will harvest later."
Og Mandino

What is your mental picture of a salesperson? Are you now ready to engage in or revamp your sales career or business? With the necessary tools and steadfast practice you can be on your way to becoming a millionaire.

Most people imagine those who have made a million dollars in sales to be extremely professional and confident. They probably sell as much because of these qualities as they do because of any experience or talent they have picked up over the years, right? Well, these are both accurate assessments.

But what about you? If you have not yet achieved a high level of success, how will you approach your first few prospects and not have them see you as the inexperienced, yet to be successful rookie you may be? How will you come across as a winner when you get face to face with a prospect? The answer is simple. *Your attitude will dictate your success*.

You're Already a Success—You Just May Not Know It Yet!

When you're serious about your career or business and are diligently applying what you're learning, then you already are on your way to being a millionaire. You simply haven't been paid that money yet because you haven't been doing it long enough. There's the small matter of putting forth the necessary effort first. But, nonetheless, you have a promissory note for that much income and more. That money is sitting in a bank waiting for you to withdraw some of it every time you go out and do your sales activities.

So what will you do the first, second, and one hundredth time you reach a prospective client, customer, or associate? You'll *act* successful. When you act like you have already made your first million—like you're already an impressive, high-powered businessperson—you will *attract* people who will buy. Even though you may not be a millionaire at this instant, prospects can tell you're in the process of being successful and they're more likely to want to be around you and do business with you. You'll have a positive influence on them. So how do you do that?

Dress the Part

The first step on the road towards professionalism is with how you dress. Suffice it to say that in business, the first impression someone gets of you is absolutely the most important one. And rarely will any prospect give you the opportunity to overcome a negative first impression.

The clothes you wear will speak volumes about you while you are waiting to get face to face with your prospect. Once you're in front of a potential client, customer, or associate, and presenting your product, services or opportunity, the prospect may not be hanging on to every word you speak with rapt attention. If you're dressed too casually or sloppily, he or she might have already decided not to buy from or associate with you before you've even begun.

The way you dress is a direct extension of how you feel about yourself and how seriously you take what you are doing. Dress down and you've immediately lowered your stature. You've made a statement about yourself and your product, service, or opportunity that says, "I take what I do casually and I'm casual about whether or not you do business with me." Dress up and others will immediately take you more seriously. You'll give the impression that you're earnest about what you do and about whether or not a prospect buys or joins your team.

A good rule of thumb in deciding how to dress would be to mirror your organization's top leaders. When you dress as they do, you are in essence telling yourself and everyone you meet that you're successful and on the road to riches.

There will often be times when you aren't face to face with a prospective client or customer. Even so, you'll immediately take your business more seriously simply by dressing like an important executive or other leader. Dressing the part will elevate your attitude and positively permeate everything you do!

You may need to go out and invest a little money in clothing, i.e., in yourself, before getting started. Some people even go to consignment shops to buy used clothes to look their best for less. And, of course, there are always sales throughout the year that you can take advantage of.

After investing that money, you'll have more at stake and you'll work harder and feel better about yourself. You'll feel like a million dollars putting on those new (at least to you) clothes, and you'll look forward to getting dressed up again. This will translate into prospects, clients, customers, and associates feeling better about you, as well. They'll immediately realize they are in the presence of someone who looks great, feels terrific about him- or herself, and values his or her career or business.

It also proves you're someone who isn't waiting to see if you can make a living in this business before committing to buying some nice things. The people you're dealing with will realize you're someone who knows where you're going and how to get there. If you have not already accumulated a professional wardrobe, purchase some clothes to fit the career or business you've chosen.

Grooming for Success

Some may say, "Clothing makes the man (or woman)." But if that person, although impeccably dressed, has not showered, shaved, fixed their hair, worn their deodorant, shined their shoes, and cleaned their fingernails, they need to do so. This may seem obvious, but apparently it isn't to everyone.

You also need to think about any jewelry you may wear. The items you might wear when socializing with friends may not always be appropriate in business. Flashy or excessive jewelry, or earrings on men, may rub some people the wrong way. And since it's just as easy to leave such jewelry at home, why take the chance that your wearing it may turn a prospect off?

Your prospects are likely to notice even the slightest thing that is amiss and you don't want anything to stand in the way of them hearing the exciting information you have to share!

So "stack the deck" in your favor. Dress and groom yourself for success. They're essential ingredients for any aspiring millionaire in sales.

Drive a Nicer Car

Just one step down on the importance ladder is the vehicle you drive. Not everyone starts off in sales with a shiny new car, and of course this is a much greater investment than a couple of new shirts or business suits. But most prospects would rather do business with someone who appears to be doing well than someone who doesn't.

If you don't think this is important, consider this scenario. What if you were striving to form a partnership with a company CEO (Chief Executive Officer)? This high-powered CEO assures you the company is on solid ground and would provide you the financial backing you need. Everything about the person seems fine, and you are put at ease by talking to him or her.

As you approach the parking lot getting ready to leave, you notice the CEO come out of the office building and get into a car so shabby and rusted that you'd be ashamed to drive it. Would you feel any different about your impending deal now? Well, prospects, clients, and customers perceive your level of success by how you present yourself, your degree of professionalism, confidence, dress, grooming, and by what you drive.

If your current vehicle isn't so great, once you've saved some money, one of the best investments you can make is to get into a better looking car. It's advisable not to go into debt—pay cash. So, if you can swing it without getting in debt, or otherwise jeopardizing yourself financially, consider buying yourself a nicer car.

Regardless of your financial situation, if your car looks a bit bedraggled, clean it up before you make even one presentation. Just cleaning the inside and washing and waxing the outside can make a big difference. And, if you have a little extra money, an inexpensive paint job can make your car look practically brand new.

A good-looking three- to five-year-old car that's already heavily depreciated could be a positive alternative. You may be surprised at how little an older luxury car costs. In fact, most are worth only half or a third as much as when they were new, yet they can still look and run like new if they have been well-maintained. If you've been buying new economy cars in the past, consider purchasing a well-kept older midsize or luxury car that you could afford to buy for the same lower cost.

Remember, that while a car is a depreciating asset, it is still a necessity. Let the previous owner take the depreciation hit until you can afford the luxury of buying a new, more expensive car. In any case, you may want to talk it over with your mentor or leader who knows your situation and can better advise you.

With a sharper looking car, as with an upgraded wardrobe, you'll feel like working harder and feel better about yourself, your company or business, and the opportunity ahead of you. Every time you leave a client, customer, or prospect and drive away in your "new" investment, you'll know you are on the road of success.

A car is often regarded as a symbol of your level of success. And make no mistake about it, the positive effect your car has on your self-esteem and other people's perceptions of you can be significant.

How Can I Get More Self-Confidence?

You may need to develop the self-confidence to go out in public, meet with people you don't know, become friends, and then convert them into customers, clients, or associates. Despite your previous background and regardless of your personality type, you can do it—when you want to badly enough. In other words, focus on your dream to keep yourself going.

Many things seem challenging when you're new to doing them. The better you get and the more success you have doing whatever it is, the easier it becomes.

No one likes to be rejected, and sales is a business that's loaded with it! No one likes to be told no, but the one who hears the most noes also hears the most yeses. The key is to keep going.

When you're prospecting and meeting new people, you never know what you're going to find. "Will they be friendly?" "Will the next one be a man, a woman, or a couple?" "Will they have a sense of humor?" "Are they straight-to-the-point people, or do they need a lot of details?" These are all questions that may run through your mind. They are also the puzzles you get to piece together every day. This not only makes your job or business fun but, as you do it, you essentially become an expert in human nature. And it's that expertise that can make you a millionaire—as long as you keep learning, growing, and persisting. Become a consummate student of sales.

So cherish the challenges each day—embrace and overcome them. Be determined to work your way through them, whatever it takes to do so. For example, if you talk with someone who isn't pleasant, learn from the experience so you can better deal with that type of person the next time you meet one.

If at First You Don't Succeed...

There may be times you encounter a prospect who, on the surface, doesn't seem to have a sense of humor. That's okay—don't let it bother you. Instead, think how fun it will be when you finally get that first hint of appreciation for your efforts. Maybe it'll be in the sparkle of an eye or crack of a smile. However it happens, you'll have gained a small reward even if you don't get a yes—something positive you can take with you. When that happens, you are becoming a master at the art of relationships—one of the biggest keys of success.

The self-confidence you need to rise to the top simply can't be turned on like flipping on a light switch. It comes through learning from your mistakes, running into obstacles, and going on, in spite of them. It involves sometimes having a challenging day and rebounding from it to have a fantastic next day—never quitting on yourself and your family.

When you realize that the rewards of turning these negatives into positives are not just short-term, i.e., the paycheck or income you receive, but long-term (meaning the person you are becoming), you'll have a greater appreciation for why you are in sales. You'll gain the most important aspect of your overall self-confidence package—self respect.

Gary, a high-level executive with a large sales company, tells about his starting out as a straight commission sales rep.

"People ask me all the time, 'What attracted you to the job when you were starting out? Why did you keep at it?' It was a long time before I actually became consciously aware of the answer, although I think I knew it all along.

"The immediate rewards I gained—more money than I had been earning, recognition, and freedom—were great. I had a lot of friends who were a few years older than I was and well established in careers like engineering or computers. Right from the beginning I was earning more than they were and, unlike them, I was able to set my own schedule entirely. That was nice. But something deeper was driving me and motivating me every day.

"Every day that I was out there cold calling, meeting people, finding their needs, and learning how to sell to them, I was also building immense character. And that's what kept me going day-in and day-out.

"Every tough situation I faced made me stronger, which enabled me to get my share of victories along the way. Week after week, I could see the development of my self-assurance, public speaking ability, and overall comfort level and sharpness around other people.

"I started off being shy and withdrawn because I was lacking self-confidence. But I soon found myself being able to meet with a prospect who was a high-powered business executive, with a lot more money than I had at the time, and look him straight in the eye and talk to him as an equal. I was actually directing him down the road I wanted him to go while I sold him my product. It was empowering to realize that no one could ever intimidate me because I knew it was my choice not to let them! And by learning to sell, I could experience some of the finer things in life that I had always wanted.

"Instead of getting up every day and pounding the pavement I knew I could easily be sitting in some air conditioned office staring at the clock until 5 p.m. and never be in control of my income or advancement. I also knew that while that may appear to be the easy way out, it was actually the harder way.

What motivated me to press on was the knowledge that not very many people have the guts to do what I was doing— even for one day—much less day-in and day-out, week after week. That made me feel special. And we all know that the people who have special talents are the most highly paid. I just knew there had to be a big payoff for going out and doing something this challenging, and I was right!"

Feel Good About Yourself and What You Do

When you endeavor to convince prospects to give you a good portion of their hard-earned money for your product or service, much of whether or not they buy depends on if they like you. And their liking you starts with you liking yourself. And you have every reason to do so. You opted *not* to take the easy road like the majority. You've decided you *can* tackle a challenging career or business not many would ever attempt, much less be successful at. And for that, you can be greatly rewarded!

Understand that your prospects, and anyone else for that matter, are no better than you, even if they are (or appear to be) wealthy with impressive job titles or degrees. They may just be very good at what they do and perhaps have been working at it for a long time. Or they may just be broke at a higher level having gone into serious debt to maintain an image of wealth—with a home and car(s) that their bank basically owns. Regardless, you are just as good as they are. And keep in mind, once you become a millionaire, you may even be richer than they may be!

Even if you're just starting out brand new in your business or career, don't ever put your prospects on a pedestal or let them intimidate you. Tell yourself that chances are they had to work hard to get where they are. Therefore they are more likely to respect the hard work you're putting in and how well you perform your job or do your business.

Also understand that they may be experts in their fields. However, in *your* field, *you* are (or are becoming) the expert. It's likely you know more about your product or service, or opportunity than they do or perhaps ever will. Therefore you can present yourself with the authority of a teacher to a pupil, or a doctor to a patient. The more self-confidence you emanate, the more trust people will have in what you share with them. It's as simple as that!

Hold Your Head Up High

Earlier we discussed the outward attitude you project. But just as important, if not more so, is the inward attitude you carry with you. This is your self-esteem—the respect you feel for yourself. You *are* perceived by how you act. And when you are with people you hope to sell to or share your opportunity with, you can behave in one of two ways.

You can choose to act small, insignificant, and unworthy. You can make little or no eye contact, turn your back to the prospect every chance you get, and mumble your words as if you hope no one hears you. You can feel as if you're not fit to be in the presence of this already successful person who has more money, a bigger home, a nicer car, and more prestige than you. But think about it. What would that behavior say about how you feel about your product, service, or opportunity? Would *you* want to buy from or associate with someone who felt that way? More importantly, would *you* want to *be* like that? No, of course not!

What you need to do, starting today, is to get in front of your prospects with all the self-confidence, ease, and grace of a veteran millionaire salesperson. When you greet these people, give them a huge smile and a strong (but not brutal!) handshake. When you speak, make eye contact and talk in a pleasing and self-assured tone.

As you present your product, service, or opportunity, do so with relaxed humor and wit. Focus on them with compassion and a loving heart—discovering their needs and wants. And even though you may be churning nervously inside, which may be natural for you, nonetheless, you'll be in command. You're sure of yourself without being cocky, and sure of your presentation without being pushy. You care about your prospects and their well-being and always encourage them to do what's best for them, assisting them however you can.

You are genuine in your compliments and determined in your resolve that you'll do everything in your power to give these people all the information and support they need to take advantage of what you're sharing. Your entire attitude will be assumptive, as if to convey the message, "You've already bought the product, service, or are interested in the opportunity. The only reason I'm here is to show you how it works and to help you take the next step." When you display an air of certainty about yourself and show sincere friendliness, you may actually feel you are halfway to the yes.

The Most Important Dinner of Your Life

Think of it this way. Imagine you're a single man and you meet the woman of your dreams. She's everything you'd ever hoped for in a woman. You fall head over heels in love, and now you want her to be your wife. She feels the same way about you; however, there's one thing standing in your way. She says you need her parents' approval before she can marry you. So she invites you over to her house for dinner to meet them. You go there with the understanding that if you're liked and accepted, the wedding is on. And if not, well, you don't want to even *think* about that!

Will you give any thought to how you're dressed that evening, or will your oldest pair of jeans and a T-shirt do? How are you going to act once you're in that house? Shy? Reserved? Nonconversant? Will you eat your dinner with your head bowed in silence and then leave the table without appropriately complimenting the cook? If you do all these things, you may as well forget about this young lady ever becoming your wife.

Instead, you would be your best self, wouldn't you? You would probably smile from ear to ear and extend your hand as you met her folks, complimenting them on their home. You would do your best to have a sense of humor, yet always with decorum and class. You would be well-groomed, dressed immaculately, and maintain excellent eye contact. You'd listen carefully to all the conversation and be attentive to where it was your place to add to it, and you would do so accordingly. You would be open and honest if her parents asked you some tough questions about what you do for a living, what your goals are, or something else. You'd respect their right to know and present yourself with integrity as someone with a great deal to offer to their daughter, which you sincerely believe you do.

Finally, when the time was right, you would ask her parents' permission for their daughter's hand in marriage and to become a part of the family. And what do you suppose the result would be? Most likely, you'd get a resounding yes!

In every presentation you make, sell yourself as well as your product, service, or opportunity. When you do, your clients, customers, and associates will welcome you into their business and personal lives much more frequently.

The First Thing You Sell Is *Yourself*

Your general attitude, how you feel about yourself, what you have to offer, how you look, where you see yourself, and *how* you see yourself are all important. These are all critical components to your overall success as a sales professional or entrepreneur. And you can fine-tune them as you go along.

Be proactive. Deliberately read personal and business development books, listen to continuing education tapes, and go to motivational/educational seminars. And *apply* what you're learning each day. Successful attributes and knowledge don't automatically come to you as a by-product of wealth and experience—although those are contributing factors. Further develop the positive aspects of your persona and work on weak areas. This can, in turn, *ensure* wealth when you persevere and approach what you're doing with an honorable intent—the integrity we discussed earlier—as you serve others.

Every day persistently work on your professionalism and self-confidence until they become habitual parts of your thinking and behavior. Duplicate what those who are leaders in your career or profession do. Take advantage of the sales tools available to you for you to use to sell effectively. And remember to keep growing personally as you go along.

Chapter Seven

$

Getting In—The Direct Approach

*"Being in the field on a daily basis and
approaching prospects who are not expecting you
is like being in a weight room for the mind."*
Brian Gotta

Sales is a simple business. Yes, and while a sales business or career can be challenging, it is truly simple. But all too many people new to sales complicate it with maintenance activities that keep them busy, but unproductive. These can be procrastination-type activities to avoid taking an action they are fearful of.

The truth is, there are only three things you really need to do every day, and all the rest is superfluous. First of all, you need to get in front of prospects. Next you need to present what you're offering, and then third, you need to close the sale. If you're discussing an opportunity instead of selling a product or service, getting the prospect to join your organization is "closing the sale."

All three steps just mentioned are very important. But getting in front of prospects is most imperative. Regardless of how great a closer you may be or how well you can share what you have to offer, if you're never in front of a prospect there will be no sale made or no associate brought in. Diligently learn and apply the first step of this trio and the other two will come easily.

What's the First Thing You Need to Learn?

There are many ways to get in front of prospects and to generate leads. Clearly, the most direct and immediate is cold calling. When you can meet new prospects and take your product or service straight to a potential client or customer without the benefit of a lead or an appointment and, with skill and finesse, start building a relationship and get into the presentation and closing phases, you can consider yourself a true sales professional.

Cold calling or canvassing is the rawest but most powerful form of lead generation there is. However, it is also the method most people least prefer to do. But once you become proficient at it, the world of opportunity opens up for you and all other lead generation methods will seem easy by comparison!

While the mission of the following three chapters is not to necessarily convince you to cold call and only cold call, much of the instruction this book gives you on being able to develop and get in front of prospects will be centered around cold calling (or as it's sometimes called canvassing or prospecting). Since every other mode of lead generation is a derivative of cold calling, learning to canvass will mean you can easily master the rest.

Brr, It's Cold!

Cold calling can be a challenging adventure, especially for new salespeople. Obviously your workday would be very pleasant if, instead of needing to prospect, your job or business consisted of coming into your office (at home or your job) and being handed three leads. Each lead would include a preset appointment containing the name and address of someone interested in seeing your product, service, or opportunity and possibly even purchasing or signing up. That would be fantastic, right?

Don't be so fast to say yes. If that's all there was to it, don't you think everyone would be doing it? And if it were that easy, would any company or corporate supplier need to pay someone a lot of money simply to show up and take an order?

The main reason sales can be so lucrative is because it *is* challenging! Anything worthwhile requires effort. Since so few people have the strength, courage, guts, or *desire* to do it, you have immediately put yourself in a very special and elite group. And that group can earn *well* above the average income and it's where many millionaires come from.

You need to face any fear you may have and jump right in so you can join that special group of highly paid people. This is not to say there aren't other effective and viable lead generation methods; it's just that if you discover something simple, direct, basic, cost effective, time efficient, and duplicatable, you need to consider doing it. Cold calling has all of these elements.

Cold calling has hundreds of positive aspects and very few negative ones. The challenge is, many people feel the negative aspects immediately and sometimes fear them more than they desire the positive outcomes. Even though most new salespeople know that cold calling is good for them, they won't do it because the fear and discomfort canvassing could cause does not in their mind seem worth the benefits it would bring. If you understand what those benefits are, and have a strong enough desire to achieve your dreams and goals, you are likely to sincerely appreciate the desirability of cold calling.

Why You Need to Do It Yourself

If you have a product or service you can take directly to a client or customer without getting anyone else involved, you've eliminated all of the middlemen, making your profit higher. The more costs involved in your getting in front of a prospective client, the less of the overall sale's margin you'll take home. So, the best way to get sales leads is to do it yourself, without involving others who would charge you for their services.

Hit the Weights

Another benefit to canvassing is the mental sharpness you gain. There is an expression used often in athletics that says, "No Pain, No Gain." If cold calling is the most challenging form of prospecting there is, wouldn't it stand to reason it's also the *best* for you?

Suppose you were going to start lifting weights. Your goal is to get in great shape and have a muscular, toned body. Would you accomplish your goal more quickly by putting five-pound weights on the bench press and exerting little effort, or by stacking on enough weight to make it hard? If every repetition burned and burned, you'd know you were doing some good.

Being in the field on a daily basis and approaching prospects who are not expecting you is like being in a weight room for the mind. Every person you meet, especially the ones who are a challenge to your positive frame of mind, is another repetition on the barbells.

Some people attempt cold calling and, after a couple of "workouts," decide it's not for them. They never go to the "gym" again. Other people, the successful ones, keep coming back and work harder each time. Emerge from this gymnasium a mental giant and you can be a financial giant as well!

The Book of Millionaires

Imagine this. Someone gives you a 20,000-page book to read. They promise that when you get to the end of the book, provided you have a basic comprehension of what it was about, then you will have permanent financial security and no money challenges. How quickly would you read that book? Would you read only a couple of pages per day, or would you read it hungrily, voraciously, cover to cover as fast as you can?

In sales, part of learning and becoming financially successful is effectively by handling prospects' objections. Every no you receive and then overcome is another page in your book, another brick in your wall, another curl of the barbell. Say you go out on one or two or three scheduled appointments, do one or two or three presentations, and then your day is done. What do you think is the most number of objections you can potentially face and then overcome that day? One or two or three! That means you chose to turn only that many pages in your book for that day.

If you cold call and get face to face with fifty prospects in a day, you might still only get three presentations for your efforts. But by bouncing back from rejection and attempting to combat fifty noes, you turned fifty pages in that book of financial security.

How do you think successful salespeople get that way? They simply talk to hundreds and thousands of people. The quicker you get hundreds and thousands of pages under your belt, the quicker you get to the end of your book *and the sooner you become financially secure!*

Power in Respect and Surprise

There are other advantages to cold calling as well. A prospect who is open to talking with you and lets you in to present yourself, without your previously setting an appointment, is likely to be more respectful of what you are doing. As mentioned earlier, he or she could be aware that what you are doing can be challenging. In fact, they may admire you for having the courage to make your living or build a strong secondary income that way. This could make them more interested in talking with and buying from you.

If you come to meet that same person on a preset appointment, he or she probably thinks you have several more leads for the day. He or she may figure somebody will surely buy from you, so there's no sense of urgency or obligation. However, if a prospect knows that telling you no means sending you "back out into the cold" and moving on to begin the whole process over again, he or she may think twice about turning you down.

There is something else often overlooked. When you cold call a prospect who didn't know you were coming, you have the elements of surprise and impulse working for you.

Think about what happens when you or someone else sets an appointment for you to do a presentation. After the appointment is scheduled, the prospect may begin to build up resistance. He or she may tell themselves over and over that they're not going to buy or get involved in anything when you come over. He or she might then mentally run down a list of all their expenses, impending or current, convincing themselves this is the worst time ever in his or her life to take on anything else.

This all builds to a crescendo right up to the moment when you arrive, smiling and happy for the opportunity to get in front of this prospect who is expecting you. As you extend your hand to greet them, they may blurt out, "I'm not buying anything!" A cold called presentation is never going to suffer from this severe disadvantage. Because the prospect was not expecting you, the buying process is much more of an emotional one, and that works heavily in your favor.

I Don't Need Any Help, Thanks—*I Can Do It Myself!*

Though there are many other advantages to cold calling too numerous to mention, there is one more we'll talk about in this chapter. The entire cold-calling process builds confidence. Say you get in front of a decision maker who wasn't expecting you, create interest where there was no interest previously, and then walk out an hour later with an order. You will gain a feeling of power, self-assurance, and downright invincibility that no one or nothing can ever diminish.

To know you can get out of your car, or pick up the phone, and then find someone who will not only hear you out, but also buy from you, is the most incredibly satisfying feeling you can know in sales. Remember that book of financial security? When you can do this, you *are* becoming financially secure forever.

If no one gives you any leads, your income is not affected. If no clients or customers call in and ask for you, your income is not touched. Anytime, in any town, you can go out, meet new people, and make not only a living, but make a fine, prosperous life. The only way you'll not be able to personally earn money is if you decide not to work. Or, perhaps there are suddenly no more people whom you can meet. I don't think so.

You have, by virtue of taking on and conquering cold calling—the greatest of all challenges in sales, secured a future for yourself and your family that no one can ever take away from you. Congratulations! You're on your way to becoming a millionaire!

Chapter Eight

$

Overcoming the Fear of Cold Calling

*"The whole trick to cold calling is to find a
few friendly, open-minded people each day who
will let you share what you have to offer."*
Brian Gotta

Why is cold calling so challenging? Why doesn't everyone want to jump right in and start making cold calls? If there are so many advantages to prospecting, why is it the most challenging thing for many salespeople to do?

If you ask most salespeople what they dislike about cold calling, they will answer that it is the "fear of rejection." No one likes to withstand the number of rejections a person could encounter in order to make one sale. But is that *really* what you fear?

That Wasn't So Bad

Let's suppose you decide to cold call and you make an approach. This is when you either pick up the phone or knock on the door and enter the place of business and introduce yourself. The prospect (usually politely) says, "No thank you," or "I'm not interested."

You just got rejected. But did that hurt? Are you going to head for the nearest corner and huddle in it crying? (If so, you'd better not count on being successful in *any* type of career or business where you deal with people.) No, the truth is it didn't bother you. The rejection isn't what you really fear. In fact, as you become a pro at cold calling, you begin to realize that you *never get rejected*.

Be the Rejecter—*Not the Rejected*

The whole trick to cold calling is to find a few friendly, open-minded people each day who will let you share what you have to offer. You may run into some people who are grouchy along the way, but frankly, it's their problem if they're not very personable—not yours. As soon as you realize you've found a less-than-friendly person or that the decision-maker is not available, don't waste your time. Instead, move on to the next prospect.

As soon as you know you won't be able to present your product, service, or opportunity, and that *your time is now being wasted*, smile and say, "Have a great day!" Then move on, rejecting *them*. Isn't that a great way of handling it? Well, it works!

When you have the proper attitude and technique as you approach people, you never get rejected. Before any prospects have the opportunity to turn you away, you part company with them.

The ability to do this is important for your self-confidence and positive attitude, but mostly it's important for your investing your time wisely. Instead of arguing with or vainly attempting to convince the wrong person, you need to be moving to the next opportunity to share what you have. In the end, whoever sees the most people, makes the most calls, and does the most presentations will make the most sales or recruit the most people.

If rejection is not what we fear, then what is? Why do so many salespeople fear cold calling and so adamantly avoid it? There are two reasons, and both are simply mental obstacles. When you can get over these two hurdles and keep on persevering, your sales career or business is going to be a great one. If you can cold call, not necessarily getting 100 percent of your business this way, but if you *can* do it, you will thrive and prosper in sales. In fact everything else you do will seem easy by contrast.

If You're Pretty Sure It Won't Work, Why Would You Try It?

The first reason for avoiding cold calling is that most people do not see the correlation between making that first call and earning any money. Before they even approach a prospect, they've convinced themselves that they have no chance of making any money by talking to strangers who are not interested and not expecting them. Therefore, why put themselves through the pain of doing it for no pay? If lifting weights didn't build muscles, do you think anyone would do it?

When a new salesperson tries cold calling for the first time without success, what was formerly a skepticism about canvassing is now a full fledged certainty—that this method of selling does not work. They can now say they tried cold calling and it's a waste of time. (Plus, that way they think they won't have to do it again and that they still can become successful in sales.)

If someone knows a specific method of marketing won't bring in any business, then of course there's no reason to use it. But if there is a method that can work when performed properly, and it's not tried simply because someone doesn't have the proper mental attitude towards it, then *that's* a mistake.

I'll Work for $20 but Not for $70!

Roger, who manages a group of outside salespeople, illustrates an example of how someone may not succeed because of his or her belief that it's not possible.

"We market our cooking products to homeowners, and a typical package we sell is priced at around $1,000. The salesperson who sells that package earns approximately $200 per sale. The average salesperson makes a sale for every three presentations he or she does.

"When I was new in the company, I primarily went door to door and was pretty good at it. I was making good money right away, and quite honestly, not working a whole lot of hours. Now that I'm a manager, it is so frustrating trying to get my salespeople to do the same thing. If we give them leads, they'll work until eight or nine o'clock at night, so I know it's not a matter of being lazy. But getting them to go out and canvass, which I know would probably earn them more money with less time away from their families, is next to impossible.

"I tried taking them out and letting them see me in the field, and some of them would get turned on for awhile. But as soon as I wasn't there to make them do it, they fell back into their old habits of coming into the office in the morning and hoping to run any lead they could rustle up just to avoid canvassing.

"One time I had a meeting with my whole group of salespeople and asked them an obvious question: 'How many of you would like to make more money and work fewer hours?' Of course every hand in the room went up.

"So next I asked them, 'How many of you feel like the reason you're not as successful as you would like to be is that you don't do as many presentations per day as you need to?' Again, almost every hand went up. I then said, 'Most all of you have been shown how to canvass for demonstrations, but how many of you don't do it because you've tried and you're not able to get in?' Same response. They all really believed that they *couldn't* get demonstrations by cold calling.

"So I picked out the newest person in the room and said, 'John, today is your third day with us, so you've never gone out and cold called. You wouldn't know the first thing about what to do, right?' He agreed. Then I took a twenty-dollar bill out of my wallet and asked, 'John, would you say you were money motivated?' He said he was.

"I continued, 'What if I made a deal with you? Starting this morning at nine o'clock I will let you go out into the field. For every prospect who will just let you step inside and show your products, even if it was only for a minute, I would pay you twenty dollars. I'd drive behind you in my car, and every time you got into a house you could come back out and I'd hand you one of these bills. You could stuff the money in your pocket and keep going. If I did that for you, how many doors would you get in?'

"With all kinds of confidence, John said 'At least five!' Some of the more veteran salespeople got excited and blurted out that for them it would be more like ten or fifteen.

"I then said, 'John would take me for at least a hundred dollars, and some of the rest of you would take me for two or three hundred.' They all wanted to do it. Then I got to what I had been leading up to.

"I said, 'Well, our closing average is one out of three. In other words, for every three houses we get into we'll make a sale, right? And our average commission is two hundred dollars. Let's say John here, because he's new, is only going to close one out of five. Five homes with a one out of five average means he'd make one sale. Five homes for two hundred dollars means he really made *forty* dollars per home, not the twenty we agreed on! And some of you, who *do* sell one out of three, said you'd go out and get into ten. Well every three presentations you do earns you $200, so you really make close to $70 per house you're in! You all said that at twenty dollars a house, you'd go out knocking on doors all day today. But for *seventy* dollars a house, it's not really worth it to canvass. Does that make any sense?

"'Yet at the beginning of this meeting, you all said you'd like to be away from home fewer hours and make more money. You also said the reason you aren't making the money is that you're not doing enough presentations. You claimed you weren't cold calling to get your business because you couldn't get in. But then you admitted that *under the right circumstances, you could get in as often as you want!*

"'I'm trying to get you to realize that you *are* under the right circumstances! There are hundreds of thousands of leads out there, if you'd realize they're just outside your car door, not in this office!' Well, that day we had one of our best days ever in volume. We still utilize other methods of lead generation, but the people who do the most cold calling are certainly our top producers."

Making Yourself Uncomfortable So You Can Win

With all of this effort devoted to convincing you that you can and need to cold call, what would stop someone from heading out right now to meet a few friendly prospects? There is another reason why ordinary salespeople don't go out and do a presentation unless given a warm, preset lead. There is one thing, above all else, that makes a salesperson hesitate to cold call and want to endeavor to find a way around it.

The real reason, which we are taught as children, and reinforced as adults, is that most people are uneasy being somewhere they don't feel welcome. We may avoid uncomfortable social situations. And even though cold calling is a business activity and not a social party, it feels very similar to being a person at a gathering who doesn't know anybody else, where you feel a little out of place and uninvited.

The truth is, no matter what you're selling, no matter how you look, and no matter how you behave, as soon as your prospects realize you're selling, their natural walls of resistance go up. And no matter how nice the prospect may be, you still can't help but feel a little bit intrusive. After all, they didn't *ask* you to come calling. The difficulty in sales is to not take that on as a personal rejection of you or your product, service, or opportunity, but simply a natural part of the territory.

This is the most challenging of any of the obstacles you can encounter when you learn to cold call. The more experience you get the more at ease you'll feel with what you're doing, and that's the most encouraging news. Remember, if it were always easy, no one would need to pay you a lot to do it.

In order to be successful, you need a strong faith and belief in your product, service, or opportunity. You need to feel like everyone needs to own it or become a part of it. Since your prospects probably don't know about what you're sharing yet, your job is to go out and educate them about the merits. If you simply waited until someone called you because you felt it would be impolite to do otherwise, you'd go out of business. Then who would gain? Your prospects probably would keep using products or services that are inferior to yours, all because you were a little too meek to share what you have with them.

Success Comes to Those Who Have Tenacity and Drive

Keep reminding yourself that you are in the weight room for building skill and talent. How do you think the greatest athletes in the world got where they are? Sure, they had some natural talent, but so do you. Yet the sports heroes you may see on TV are not all necessarily the men and women gifted with the most athletic ability, just like the most highly paid salespeople in the world did not necessarily have the most raw, innate skill to begin with.

What these athletes and salespeople have in common is tenacity and persistence—they have a burning desire. For every pro sports star with a multi-million-dollar contract, there were probably a thousand others coming out of high school at the same time with equal or greater athletic gifts. They simply weren't willing to pay the price for success. You either choose to pay the price of success or you *will* pay the price of failure. So why not go the extra mile?

When they're tired of practicing, the greatest basketball players shoot two hundred more jump shots. When they're exhausted and their hands are sore, the best hitters in baseball take another hundred pitches in the batting cage. For every great touchdown reception you see a star receiver make in front of a roaring crowd, there were five hundred more made the week before in front of no one. And before that, there were hundreds of thousands of catches in junior high, high school, and college.

Whenever they weren't practicing their sport, these superstars were in the real weight room. They were pushing themselves farther than they thought they could be pushed, putting themselves through tortures no one ever sees or writes about in the sports page. They disciplined themselves this way because they had a dream, and they knew that pain today meant glory tomorrow.

What about millionaire salespeople? Do you think they got where they are on their looks, charm, and speaking ability? No. They got there because when they were tired and felt like quitting, they knocked on just *one* more door. When all of the other salespeople in their organization were at the coffee shop in the evening swapping stories, they were on the telephone wrapping up the last deal or on an appointment they couldn't get to in the afternoon. They were focused on their goal and they were squeezing every last ounce of potential out of that day.

When they were cold calling, facing rejection after rejection, questioning why they were putting themselves through this on a daily basis, they remembered there was a reason. They were practically getting a Ph.D. in Psychology. They were pouring through the book of millionaires as if someone might take it away from them tomorrow, so they felt they had better read it today! They knew that by doing something few people are willing to do, they were building character, building their mental muscles, and making themselves superstars.

Come Out of the Locker Room—It's Game Time!

So you want to be a millionaire? You want to have the fun and exciting life you feel you deserve? Then go out and pay a price. Get to the end of *your* book of millionaires before it's too late. Just like everyone else who is successful, you'll have times of self-doubt, times you'll be low, and times when you think you can't do it and may as well quit.

Just remember the roar of the crowd that's driving you. Your moment of glory may not be nationally televised. There will be no front-page articles in the newspaper when you win. The thunderous ovation from the stadium will be audible only to you.

But you won't have to wait a week to hear it on game day. You'll hear it each time you pay the mortgage on your family home, perhaps adding some extra to the principle to pay it off early—and each time you put away some more money for your children's college education or your retirement. You'll hear it each time you look in your children's eyes and realize that because of you they will have a better, more prosperous life. You are showing them how they can win in life too. Because you didn't take the easy way out, you'll know something few know when you look in the mirror. You'll know that you have done and will continue to do the very best you can within your ability. Congratulations—*you're* becoming a superstar.

Chapter Nine

—$—

How to Cold Call

*"How you respond to a prospect's initial rejection is
the key to how you'll do in sales. You need to be ready for
some initial rejection several times a day."*
Brian Gotta

Now that you've got the courage and self-assurance to go out and meet people who don't know you, what do you say when you meet them? Fortunately, the proper approach is so basic that virtually anyone can learn to do it. But get ready to toughen yourself up. The only way you ever get great at cold calling is to practice and be willing to suffer the possible challenge of making an unskilled approach where you feel disappointed with the results. That is how you learn, though. So be patient with yourself. Become a champion at cold calling and you could make a *lot* of money. Persevere, persevere...*persevere!*

A winning approach has many components, and you need to invest time to learn the best way to cohesively incorporate all of them so a prospect wants to listen to you. It's natural to think you sound terrible at first, but remember, these prospective clients, customers, or associates have probably never heard such an approach before, so they don't know if it's great or not. No matter how little you may know about your product, service, or opportunity, rest assured, you likely know more than they do!

Look in the Mirror

The first and most important aspect of a terrific approach may be obvious. You need to project that you're happy and friendly. As soon as you understand that virtually every prospect is like a mirror, reflecting back to you whatever it is you give off, you'll begin to fear rejection less and less.

Do you want a stranger who's meeting you for the first time to be grumpy and angry? Then make sure you're stone faced, sullen, and looking like you're having a miserable time. Don't speak with confidence, but rather with fear in your voice, and make sure you seem ready to argue. You're then sure to get a response that reinforces your belief that all prospects don't like salespeople. You'll believe that a face-to-face meeting of a new prospect is ancient, prehistoric, and doesn't work in today's high-tech society. But the truth is, the more technological tools we have at our disposal, the more people need to have the personal touch.

People generally enjoy being with others who are pleasant and brighten their day. Be one of those people and you'll greatly increase your chances of success. Meet your prospect with a huge smile and a sparkle in your eyes. Act like you are having the most fun you've ever had, regardless of how you may be quaking inside. Speak up clearly, with vibrancy in your voice and confidence in your demeanor. Be friendly. The prospect usually can't help but reflect your attitude. Hey! If this idea is one you're just beginning to incorporate, go out and find your first friendly prospect! That's a fine start.

Of course, you can't just stand there smiling at your prospects and expect them to read your mind and know you want to share something with them. If you would like to get their permission to present your product or service, you need to begin your approach. If you're prequalifying them to share your opportunity, then it's questioning and relationship-building time. Follow whatever you've been taught in both cases. Do what the leaders in your business do to get excellent results.

The next several pages cover a basic approach that can be used when talking to any new prospect about a product, service, or opportunity. In your particular situation, it may not be appropriate to ever actually knock on a prospect's door unannounced.

However, in any business there are aspects of cold calling. Every time you meet new people you use approaches similar to a door-to-door salesperson. Read the following section with an open mind while asking yourself, "How does this apply to my situation?" You're likely to find more similarities than you may now think.

Since most people you'll meet are busy, if you're presenting your product or service, it's important you get to your point immediately and state your intentions.

The first thing you may want to say is some kind of an ice-breaker. Make a quip about yourself or ask a question that may be a little off center, and the prospect may immediately smile. But don't dwell on this. Your prospects are busy and so are you, so get into the approach about your product or service as soon as possible. The basic steps you need to follow are:

1. Introduction.
2. Ask a question.
3. Explain why you're there.
4. State how much time you're requesting.
5. Make the break.
6. Agree with the objection and continue.
7. Repeat steps 3-5.

Introduction

Quickly introduce yourself and your company to the prospect. The fewer platitudes the better. Don't waste a lot of time with questions like, "How are you today?" You had better get to the point quickly because you're running out of time. Plus this question practically invites the response, "Busy"!

Ask a Question

Ask an unrelated question such as "Have you ever heard of (company name)?" This could let you know immediately what you are up against. Sometimes you'll draw out an objection right here. But that's alright. Just proceed.

This question is often helpful because it is so unexpected. Most customers are not well versed in any type of sales approach (giving you a huge advantage). They figure you're just going to come out and ask, "Would you like to buy (whatever your product or service is)?" In that case, they may figure an easy no will get rid of you. But by starting with a question the client or customer doesn't expect, the element of surprise sometimes buys you just enough time to continue. Steps three through seven are the meat of your approach.

Explain Why You're There

You're obviously there for a reason. Don't attempt to kid anyone that you don't hope to gain something for putting yourself through the rigors of cold calling. Those who answer the door or phone immediately will probably suspect you want into their wallet. What you *tell* your clients or customers you're hoping to win over makes all the difference if you want to show them what you have to share.

Instead of immediately telling your prospects you want to sell them something, you need to ask them if you can do a presentation, which is much less of a threat. The interest in your product or service can come later.

If you tell your prospects, "My company asked me to get consumer feedback for advertising," or "The company pays me to show it to you," or "I get credit for showing it to folks for advertising," or "I'm here to get your opinion on what I've got to share with you," then you've deflected the spotlight away from your being just another "salesperson." Just be sure to be honest in the process. (For example, it's true that out of "x" number of cold calls, you're likely to get "y" number of yeses. So, yes, your company or supplier corporation does pay you a commission or a bonus on the yeses!)

State How Much Time You're Requesting

Mention a brief period of time you'll need. If you leave this step out, your prospects may automatically assume the worst and imagine you taking up the rest of their afternoon. Say something such as, "It'll just take a second," or "It only takes five minutes," or "If you could just answer five quick questions, I'll be done." This way you eliminate some of the apprehension your prospects may have about you eating away at their precious time.

Also, if you mention that there are a certain number of people you still need to talk to before the day (or evening) is over, you solidify your claim that you are not looking for a lot of time. In fact, say something like, "I still need to show it five more times today," or "I need three more people to sign this opinion form." You'll come across as being in such a hurry that no one will think you'll be wasting their time. And while you won't get any charity, it doesn't hurt that some people may even want to let you make your presentation because they feel good helping a hardworking person like you reach your daily goal.

Make a Break

Making a break is one of the most necessary steps in the process. The break you make can be subtle, almost imperceptible, and your doing one will determine whether or not you move on to the next step—the presentation. Making a break is the difference between needing to work all day (or evening) just to get one presentation, or instead spending very little of your day or evening not actually in front of a prospect. (The more you are face to face with a prospect, the more likely you are to reach your goals—as you go through the numbers.)

Making a break, in a nutshell, is the act of assuming you are being given permission to share what you have. You can have the greatest verbal approach in the world, but if you stand still and quiet, expecting to receive permission, you may be disappointed. Some examples of making a break are as follows. Remember, an assumptive attitude and confidence are the keys.

First we've introduced ourselves to the prospect, said what we do or who we represent (only if you may correctly call yourself a representative—in some cases, depending on your supplier company, this is prohibited), asked if he or she has heard of us, and perhaps mentioned we've been asked to get opinions on our product or service. This can work when sharing an opportunity too. Then we said we're only asking for a couple of minutes, but that we need to do five presentations today. At this point we break.

If the break needs to be away, such as to your car, you'll make a motion over toward your vehicle and say, "I'll just get my demo kit which has some information for you (or say whatever is appropriate to what you are presenting); and I'll be right back." If you start to walk away and the customer or client doesn't stop you, keep going because you've just gotten permission to make your presentation!

Another example may be that you motion back behind your prospect and say, "How about if we just go into your office (or sit down—whatever is appropriate) real quick." Then lead them to go in the direction you want by taking a little step forward, not aggressive but very subtle, which says to your prospect, "You've already given me permission. I expect to be invited in, so let's go!" Chances are good your prospect will make the identical move you make and lead the way.

Notice the intricacies of the break. *Never* did we ask permission. We assume we have it. You could use almost identical words, but if you ask instead of tell, you'll get a negative response every time. For instance; "Is it okay if I run out to my car and get some information for you?" or "Would you mind if we went into your office so I can show you what I've got to offer?" You've just given your prospect the perfect opportunity to say no.

This isn't to say you *can't* ask a question to make a break. For whatever it is you're sharing, there are many different ways to approach the person—different phrases and different breaks. It's the lack of confident body language and attitude that makes the prospect say no. Some people virtually whimper and are very shy—which elicits a no. Act confident, even if you're not, and your chances are improved enormously of getting to share what you have to offer. Have good eye contact, a firm handshake, and a smile. Practice this in front of a mirror, or with your mentor or leader, until you get it right.

Think of it another way. If you go to a doctor because you have an illness, the doctor doesn't say to you, "Would you mind taking this prescription every day to get rid of it?" Instead, the doctor says, "You'll take two of these each day with meals. That should clear it up, but come back and see me in a week for another exam."

In most cases, you would unquestioningly leave the office and do what the doctor said to do. If you ever heard a doctor such as in the first example, you'd probably leave his or her office and never return because he or she would sound uncertain of what they're saying—planting seeds of doubt in your mind. Even though the diagnoses were the same, the difference was the doctor's confidence.

Now you've made your break. You've confidently assumed that anyone would let a hard working, friendly, and happy individual like you to do a presentation! You're all set, right?

No. You're only halfway through your first page of this book of becoming a millionaire. The customer or client could still say, "I'm not interested," or "I don't have time right now," or "I already have one that's just fine."

They Said No, but Do They Really Mean It?

How you respond to a prospect's initial rejection is the key to how you'll do in sales. You need to be ready for some initial rejection several times a day. Don't internalize it or argue with it—instead *overcome* it! You'll be fine as soon as you understand that these phrases are not personal attacks; they're nothing more than the prospect's *reflex*.

Chances are your prospects didn't even hear what you said. All they heard was "Hi! I'm blah, blah, blah, blah, blah, blah, blah, blah, blah." And then, as soon as they heard a pause in the "blahs," they said, "No thank you." You could respond by saying, "Did you actually hear what I just said?" and they'd say back, "I don't care; I'm not interested!"

You can find a great illustration of how true this is when you go into a retail store. Let's suppose you walk into a clothing store knowing you need to buy something. In fact, you're sure you're going to buy something. As you enter, the clerk approaches you and says, "May I help you?" Even though you know what you want, have money in your wallet, and are ready to buy, what do you almost invariably say? *"I'm just looking."* In other words, "Get lost!"

However, the fact is, you're *not* just looking—you're buying! Yet out of reflex, you tell the clerk to go away, (which, by the way, he or she usually obediently does). Then when you find what you want, you're kicking yourself because the clerk is off helping someone else, and you have to stand around to get someone to wait on you. How many times have you replayed that scenario? Probably lots!

So now, here you are getting your initial rejection. And just like everyone else in that retail clothing store, the client or customer has instinctively fended off your first approach with a polite, "I'm not interested." No problem. This is where you're going to differentiate yourself from the run of the mill, ordinary sales clerk who is paid a mediocre wage, needs someone to come to him or her in order to make a sale, and scurries off at the first sign of any resistance. Now is when you make your approach again.

Agree With the Objection and Continue

Wake up your prospects. Be sure they hear *what you actually say*, rather than just the sound of your voice. As soon as a prospect says the word "interested," you agree.

Prospect: "I'm not interested."

You: "Oh, I'm sure you're not. It's just like I said, I get advertising credit for showing it. It'll only take a minute, and I still have to do it three more times today (motion in or away). I'll just set it up over there."

This is a repeat of steps three through five. If the reflex objection was "I don't have time right now," your response is almost the same—"Oh, that's fine. But like I said, it just takes a minute, and I still have to do it three more times today. I'll just step inside there (break as you motion ahead and take a small step forward) and be real quick."

At this point, if you still haven't been given permission, you have three options, and you need to make a decision instantaneously. The more experience you have the more accurate and immediate your judgments will be, but your choices are....

1. Make another approach. If there seemed to be any opening, any hesitation, any cracks in the client's or customer's staunchness of objection, then the third time might be a charm. Say the same thing with a little different wording so you don't sound like a robot. Wouldn't it be awful if one more approach was going to result in a presentation and maybe even a huge sale, but you were too meek to attempt it?

Hint: When you're brand new, you really have no foundation to base your judgment on regarding whether you need to make a third or even fourth approach. However, by giving up every time after two attempts and telling yourself "The prospect said no and meant it," you'll walk away from hundreds of sales or recruits you were only one approach from gaining. And that would be a shame.

The only way to learn which clients or customers are to be given another chance and which ones aren't is to push a little too much a few times and find out the hard way. This may not be the most pleasant thing to do but, you've come this far so, you know there will be some growing challenges involved in the process of becoming a more successful salesperson. This happens to be one of them. You'll probably need to unintentionally irk a few people at first in order to find out how far you can go and where to draw the line. Just remember, this is business—*it is not personal*. Value the lessons you learn. Even though you may occasionally irritate a prospect, the option of making yet another approach is usually the best choice.

2. Attempt to book an appointment. If lack of time was the objection given after both approaches, maybe the client or customer has some interest in what you're offering but legitimately is tight on time at the moment. If you sense this may be the case, offer an appointment for later. Say, "I know you're really busy right now. But I *am* going to be back in this area again on Friday. How about I come back then? (Don't pause and wait for a response here, keep talking). I have an opening at 10:30 a.m. and at 4:30 p.m. Which of those is better for you?"

There are two things to keep in mind about booking the appointment. One is that *the best time for you to present your product or service is now, not in the future.* If you book an appointment for later, the client or customer may choose to avoid you and not be there at the scheduled time. Typically known as a "no-show," this behavior is rude and most prospects won't treat you this way. Nonetheless, it is a risk you need to deal with. To help you avoid a "no show," you can add, "If something comes up, give me a call and we can reschedule. And I'll do the same." Then, as you leave, say, "See you Friday at 10:30!"

One more thing about setting appointments: Sometimes, if you're clever, you can use setting an appointment as an actual approach to sharing what you've got right then. Once the prospect has agreed to a set time and date in the future, he or she might, with a little prompting from you, just decide to go ahead and get it done today.

This could occur if you say to the client or customers, "You know, I do have an appointment in 25 minutes. But if you have a couple of minutes, I wouldn't mind showing you real quick what I've got to offer right now." Oftentimes this is all that is required for the client or customer to soften and then yield. An hour and perhaps a yes later, you realize that maybe the prospect wasn't so pressed for time after all. Ninety percent of the time, what clients or customers say at first is not true; it's just reflex. This is key.

3. Your third option, after repeating the approach various ways and several times and possibly even going for an appointment to get together, is to simply move on. This is where you become the rejecter, not the one being rejected. The moment you realize you're wasting your time with a prospect who is unwilling to let you proceed, cut your losses and go on to the next one. The great thing about cold calling is that there are an infinite number of prospects to whom you can talk, so it is okay if some people are not receptive. You just keep going, that's all.

Since sales is a numbers game, you need to be concerned with time (activity) management. If you approach fifty people every day while another salesperson or associate approaches only twenty-five, you're likely to earn at least twice as much money as they do! Therefore, the more quickly you can move on to the next prospect, regardless of what the last one said, the sooner you'll get to a yes.

Have a great day! You gave it your best shot. You left the prospect on an excellent note and then got ready for the next one. Always be kind and courteous, no matter what.

No One Can Affect Your Attitude—*Unless* You Let Them

Remember, *always* leave the prospect, client, or customer in a polite and professional manner, *regardless* of how he or she may treat you. If someone has a negative attitude, don't ever give them the satisfaction of dragging you down. Keep your positive, "I will succeed in spite of any and all adversity," attitude at all times.

If you show that you are annoyed or upset, if you say something sarcastic or mean in return, you just let the client or customer who is feeling grouchy negatively affect you. And worst of all, you hurt yourself because you may let it bother you on your next approach.

If you feel the desire to retaliate for any mistreatment you encounter, do so by responding with even more pleasantness. You'll come to understand that nothing frustrates irritable clients or customers who have a mean disposition more than their realization that they can't do anything to affect your cheery disposition!

As you walk away with your big smile and happy, confident gait, you motivate yourself by thinking, "Thank goodness, I'm me! If I had that miserable attitude, I'd never get where I'm going. I hope, for their own sake, that they learn to have an optimistic attitude."

The Mechanics of the Approach

Let's consider Joe, who sells thermal windows. When the Schilling Company hired him, he was asked to go out cold calling and see if he could get homeowners to sign up for an installation of the new, energy-efficient windows Schilling manufactured. Joe was eager and excited about his product, but the way he went about promoting it just wasn't working for him.

After two days in the field, his boss asked him how things were going. Joe admitted that he hadn't had one customer agree to let him perform an estimate.

When Joe's boss asked to hear his approach, he learned that Joe was asking everyone at the door if they would be interested in saving hundreds of dollars on their heating bills by purchasing new windows. And while that question seemed reasonable to Joe, the only thing his prospects perceived when they met him was that here was a man at the door who wanted to sell them something. And they weren't interested.

A New Approach
Joe's boss asked him to do something different. "Joe," he said, "I'll tell you what. All I'd like you to do is go out today and get five people to let you give them an estimate—don't even try to sell. If you can get five people to let you inside their houses to see what they need from us, I'll pay you whether or not any of them ends up buying."

The rest, as they say, is history. The next day, when Joe simply asked to do a courtesy estimate with no obligation to buy, he had his five price quotes completed by noon. He learned that he couldn't ask for the sale before he made a presentation, and so the first step was to be allowed to present the product, the next step was to build interest, and then, and only then, could he ask for the order.

Now Joe is one of Schilling's top sales reps and here are some samples of approaches he uses in the field when calling on residential prospects:

(Doorbell rings; prospect answers.)

Joe (smiling): "Hello. I'm Joe with the advertising department of Schilling Windows. Have you ever heard of us before?"

Prospect: "No, I haven't."

Joe: "That's fine. I'm here because we've got a new energy-saving product on the market, and my company has asked me to get consumer feedback on its value to customers. It takes just five minutes, but I need to get five opinions today. So (motioning in the house behind the customer and stepping forward slightly), I'll just give you a quick idea of what we have."

Prospect (opening the door): "Alright but I'm not buying anything."

Wow! That was easy, you may be thinking. At this rate Joe could have his five presentations and maybe even two or three sales by noon! But if it was really always that easy, it wouldn't pay so well, would it? The truth is, there *will* be some times where that's all there is to it, but they're the exceptions not the rule. Let's look at another approach:

(Doorbell rings; prospect answers.)

Joe: "Hello. I'm Joe with the advertising department of Schilling Windows. Have you ever heard of Schilling?"

Prospect: "I'm not sure. What are you selling?"

Joe: "Well, I'm here because we've got a new energy-saving product on the market, and I get credit for just getting opinions on its quality. It only takes a couple of minutes, but I need four more credits today (make a break). I'll just show you real quick—."

Prospect: "The windows I have are fine. I'm all set, but thank you."

Joe: "Oh, I'm sure you don't want to buy anything, but like I said, I get credit for just showing you what we have. This way if you ever are in the market maybe you'll keep us in mind. I still need to show four more today (break), and it'll only take a minute."

Prospect: "Alright (opening door), I'll give you a minute. But I'm in a hurry."

Joe got in again! He's on roll. (By the way, this client, who was in such a hurry, let him do an hour-long presentation!) Can Joe keep the momentum going?

(Doorbell rings; prospect answers.)

Joe: "Hello. My name's Joe. I'm with Schilling W—."

Prospect: "No thanks."

Joe: "As I started to say, I'm with Schilling Windows advertising and—."

Prospect (sternly): "I'm *not* interested."

Joe: "Thank you for your time. Have a great day!"

Here was a case where Joe quickly realized he was getting nowhere. His job is to find five *friendly* people per day who would listen. This prospect didn't fit that description. Joe could have argued that the prospect didn't even know what he was offering yet. He could have been curt with a sarcastic comment such as "Not interested in what?" Both of these responses would have served only to waste Joe's time and possibly damage his attitude as well as, perhaps, the reputation of the company he works for.

Instead he made the bright choice. He separated himself from the situation with politeness, let it go, and didn't think about it again the rest of the day. He figured since his first two calls were so easy, he was due for one like that anyway, and it cost him a total of 35 seconds. No big deal.

The minute you dignify an unfriendly person by lowering yourself to his or her attitude, you've lost—time, money, and your professionalism. No one wins. People with negative attitudes can be a waste of your time, so be pleasant and move on. If you want to get back at them in some way for being unkind, remember this: *Success is the best revenge*.

The next time Joe found a prospect at home, he was determined to give it his best shot. (He decided to knock on the door this time; prospect answers.)

Joe: "Hello sir. I'm Joe from the advertising department of Schilling Windows. I bet you were hoping I'd come by today."

Prospect (smiling back at Joe): "You bet wrong!"

Joe: "I'm just joking with you. I'm here because we've got a new energy-saving window that we're gathering some opinions on. And I get credit just for having you look at a sample. I need to show it three more times today and it only takes a couple of minutes (starts to hand his sample to the prospect). If I can just have you take a look at this."

Prospect: "I'm really busy right now. I don't have time for it."

Joe: "That's great because it takes just a couple of minutes for you to look at them. Then you just sign the questionnaire, and I'll be done and out of here. But I'd really appreciate it, and I still have three opinions to get."

Prospect: "Like I said, I'm busy right now. If you want to come back another time, I might be able to help you then."

Joe: "Okay. I appreciate that, and I don't want to hold you up. I'm going to be in area again on Thursday on a call. How about I stop by at 2 and just have you look at a sample real quick?"

Prospect: "You know, I'm not going to be interested in any windows, so there's no need for you to come back and waste your time."

Joe: "Believe me, it won't be a waste of time. Since I have to show five samples a day, and I'm going to be out here that day anyway, I'd just as soon show one to a friendly person like you. Can you squeeze in a couple of minutes at 2?"

Prospect: "Alright. It's up to you."

Joe: "Great. I'll just put you down in my book here. Thursday is the twenty-eighth. You're at 3445 Oak Street. That's at 2 p.m. Your name?"

Prospect: "I'm Stan Perry."

Joe: "Okay, Mr. Perry. I really appreciate you helping me out. I'll be back by day after tomorrow at 2 p.m., and I'll only keep you a couple of minutes, okay?"

Prospect: "Okay. Goodbye."

Joe got an appointment for Thursday. When he left, he had mixed feelings about what happened. He was glad for an appointment. Judging by the home Mr. Perry lived in, if he got in there on Thursday, Joe was very confident he would have a sale. But Joe also felt that while booking the appointment he could have just asked *one* more time to go ahead and show it today, and that Mr. Perry would have let him. Now Joe worried there was the possibility the customer may forget the appointment between now and then, or just choose to avoid it.

However, Joe also knew that even if he got no answer at Mr. Perry's door on Thursday it wouldn't be a big deal. Joe planned on working this neighborhood all day Thursday anyway. If he got in this one, then great. If not, there are plenty more "Mr. Perrys" to call on.

Joe looked at his watch. It was only 11:30 a.m. and he already had two shows and an appointment for later. A good start. His goal was to have two presentations before lunch and then three more after. Joe was right on schedule.

The next prospect who answered was a very friendly lady with a nice smile, but she turned out to be a little more of a challenge than Joe expected.

Joe: "Hi! I'm Joe from Schilling Windows advertising. Have you ever heard of Schilling?

Prospect: "No. You've got a tough job, and I admire you for it. But I'm not interested."

Joe: "It's not so tough when I get to talk to nice people like you all day. I just talked to Mr. Perry down the street. He's real nice too. Do you know him?"

Prospect: "Oh yes, I know Stan. Did he buy something from you?"

Joe: "No, I'm with the advertising department of Schilling and they've asked me to get opinions on our products. It only takes a couple of minutes, but I still have three more to show (break). How about I just get you to take—."

Prospect (as she cuts him off in mid-sentence): "I'm not interested. No thank you."

Joe: "I know you're not interested, and that's fine. It only takes a couple of minutes, though, and we're hoping if you ever are in the market you'll think of us (pointing behind the customer). Do you have many windows on that side of the house?"

Prospect: "I'm very busy right now, and I just don't want to take the time. Thank you for coming over though."

Joe: "Mr. Perry said that you were the nicest lady on the block and that I should definitely come and see you."

Prospect: "Oh, I *bet* he did, sure."

Joe: "Like I said, it will only take a couple of minutes."

Prospect (smiling): "I don't *have* a couple of minutes, and I'm not going to be interested."

Joe (smiling back): "You don't *need* to be interested, and I could have already gotten my credit five minutes ago. Just take a quick look at these (motion inside).

Prospect: "Even if I was interested, I couldn't buy anything. It's not a good time."

Joe: "How about if I just show you these, and then I'll be out of your hair?" (another motion inside).

Prospect: "Okay. You've got two minutes."

Joe got *much* more than two minutes! By the time he showed Mrs. Walker how much money he could save her with his product and, by giving her a great deal on the package she needed, he closed a terrific sale 90 minutes later. It turns out that Mrs. Walker had been thinking about getting some new windows for several months, but she had never actually done anything about it.

When Joe left, his new customer was very happy. She had taken care of a project that had been in the back of her mind for quite a while. She felt good about her purchase, the deal she got, and the service she would get with Schilling Windows.

Joe felt great, too. Not only because he made some money on the sale, but also because he had provided his new client with something she really needed, and at a better value than any of his competitors would have.

But the best thing about the whole process was that Mrs. Walker really was a nice lady, and Joe felt it was enjoyable and a privilege to have met her. (Like all businesses, when you get right down to it, sales is a people business. It's the people who matter. And they give you both the joy, as well as the challenges, to grow through.)

Later Joe reflected on what had transpired at her door. When he was brand new to sales, Joe would have given up after the first attempt when the prospect said she wasn't interested. But as he gained some experience, Joe began to notice little things that, in this case, really paid off.

For instance, the first thing Mrs. Walker said to him was that she knew he had a tough job and she admired him for doing it. This told Joe that Mrs. Walker respected a hardworking, friendly, and positive person like him, which gave him the encouragement to persist with her.

Joe also noticed that she didn't stick with one clear objection. Her reasons for not letting him in jumped from no time, to no interest, to no money. As a sales rookie, this would have seemed like three punches in the stomach. What he learned, as he gained experience, however, was that *the only true objections are the ones repeated over and over*. Since she didn't use one and only one, all three must have been smokescreens.

But the main reason Joe hung in with the approach was that he was smiling throughout his discourse, and Mrs. Walker was smiling back. There was instant rapport between them. For Joe to walk away from that would have been a mistake. When Joe left her house at 1:30 p.m., having already made more money for the day than most people make in three days, and having made a new friend in the process, he was convinced he had the best job in the world.

Summing Up the Approach

When you cold call, always remember the following points. First, keep in mind that cold calling is the most basic, direct, and cost efficient method of acquiring new prospects. It can also be the most challenging to do. But your ability to master any or all other methods of lead generation will be greatly enhanced by your expertise at cold calling.

As this book moves forward into other forms of lead generation, notice that all approaches contain the same components, no matter how they are done. The objective is always to get the presentation—nothing else. Selling during an approach is a prescription for failure, and you need to fight off any urge to do so.

They Don't Always Mean What They Say

Also remember that objections are generally reflexes—not legitimate facts. This is another reason why you need to focus on one goal only: Show what you have to offer. Don't be concerned if the client or customer says he or she has no time or money and that you'd be wasting your time. Get in, find a way to share what you have, and get the prospect interested, and soon you are likely to find out there is some time or money there after all! It's amazing how the time and money can "magically appear" once the prospect is interested in what you have to share.

You don't care if the person says he or she has no time. Get him or her to listen to you and let your personality, charm, and genuine interest in people take over. It can quickly become apparent that you have as long as you want to make a great presentation!

You also don't care if the prospect tells you he or she is not interested. Your job is to find people who *aren't* initially interested—more so even than people who are. You get paid so well because anyone can sell to someone who *is* interested. Whereas, it takes some skill and a great attitude to go out of your comfort zone and get people who previously weren't thinking about it to buy from or associate with you.

An important part of your approach is not something you *say*; rather, it's something you *project*. When you smile, convey friendliness, and a nonthreatening calm self-confidence, prospects will not only want to treat you well, but also be more likely attracted to whatever it is you have to offer.

You're in a Hurry!

Speak quickly. Joe got his words out fast. He used phrases such as "real quick" and "only takes a couple of minutes" over and over again. When he spoke, it was as if he had places to go and needed to get there immediately. He wasn't just out passing time in the neighborhood. Instead, he conveyed a sense of urgency.

If you act as if you're in a hurry, the client or customer will be more likely to let you share what you have. Why? Because generally they fear that once you started talking about what you're sharing, you'll keep them from what they had been doing for a long time. You'll camp out all day until you either get a yes or they have to ask you to go.

But when you say it only takes a few minutes and that you still need to make "x" number of presentations today, you communicate the message, "The faster I can get in and get out, the faster I get to go home." Now the prospect doesn't think you're even interested in staying long, because it would slow you down in your pursuit of your daily goal.

But if you talk in a monotone, slowly, with no vibrancy in your voice, repeating the same phrases over and over without feeling or friendliness, no one will want to let you share what you've got to offer. If you appear boring, depressed, dejected, or if you seem not to be in any hurry, the prospect has no reason to believe you will behave any differently if you came in.

Stay Positive

Don't argue or get upset with the people you're talking to, no matter how justified you may be. They win and you lose if you get irritated. On the other hand, you win if you meet their hostility with a smile that looks as if you feel they just paid you the highest compliment you've ever been paid. They can choose to win if they want to, and respond with equal friendliness. But they may just choose to be frustrated, instead!

As you walk away, turn any negative into a positive. That person just helped you become stronger. You just proved to yourself that you have a positive attitude that cannot be shaken. The fact that your friendliness was met with anger only shows that the prospect isn't very happy and possibly dislikes *you* for being so happy.

Put your faith in the numbers. When you teach yourself that every day your only goal is to do a certain number of presentations, regardless of the results, you'll find it all much easier and more pleasant. You cannot control who says yes, but you *can* better control how many times you make a presentation. Concentrate on what you *do* control, not on what you don't. Wake up each day and say to yourself, "I'm going to make "x" number of presentations today." This way you've set a goal for yourself that you know you'll do your level best to attain, no matter how little or much time it takes.

It is likely there are still more pointers you need to learn about face-to-face cold calling, but they come with experience. Anyone can learn to cold call well when he or she has the desire to do so. The first week or so may be challenging, as you put your new skills into practice. You may even question whether you *can* do it, *should* do it or even *want* to do it. Your pay may be low, while your doubt may be high. You may be working harder than you've ever worked in your life. So what? Keep persisting. You're soon likely to see progress as you fine-tune your approach, and then you won't want to wait to start as you'll greet each day with excited anticipation. And you'll be so fired up you'll want to finish this book so you can get out there and learn more!

Chapter Ten

§

Referrals

*"In the final analysis of any sales
position or business, referrals are the
real secret to increasing success."*
Brian Gotta

Besides cold calling, what other lead generation methods are effective? Anything that puts you in contact with a prospect is worthwhile. The best way to evaluate whether or not a particular method is beneficial is to weigh its cost (in time, money, and effort) against its results. One thing is for sure, if you don't want to cold call 100 percent of the time but still want to succeed in sales, you need to learn some alternate lead generation methods. The biggest mistake any salesperson could make is to wait around for someone else to provide a qualified lead. It is your responsibility, not anyone else's!

Why Ask For Referrals?

The art of gaining referrals is the other true and basic form of lead generation. Getting referrals requires diplomacy and persistence. Often, clients or customers are hesitant to give them. But when you are serious enough about acquiring referrals and you understand their importance and potential, you can soon become an expert at referred selling.

Watch Your Business Grow

Referrals have two main advantages. First, the number of referrals available is unlimited. Second, any presentation you do from a referral is one you didn't have to cold call to get. A referral call is a warmer, more relaxed call, because right from the start you and the client have something in common—a mutual acquaintance who is your referring customer. This is clearly advantageous because you immediately can make a friend with your new prospect by discussing matters other than business—right off the bat.

A smart salesperson will treat this new prospect much differently than a cold-called client. With this person you'll be able to break the ice (and won't have as much ice to break) by rolling a fair amount of information and fact-finding into otherwise just pleasant conversation. You'll want to talk about the person who referred you. If they're friends, find out how long they've known each other and other pleasant details about the two of them. This all helps to establish you as more of a friend than a salesperson as you build rapport more easily.

At the same time you'll begin casually mentioning the particulars of what you did when you made your presentation to the original customer and how well it was received. This is also your opportunity to introduce your objective. And finally, remembering that the lifeblood of your business is your future customer base, you can begin to subtly suggest that you will be asking for more referrals.

There are many salespeople who make their living solely on referral sales. Most people instantly understand why this is the case. Imagine it's your first day in your new sales career or business. What would happen if your only goal on each presentation you did that day was to get ten referrals?

Some of the time you may get everything you ask for. Then there will be other times when you won't. So if you make three presentations and from each you ask for ten referrals, you may get five a piece. However, five times three clients equals fifteen new prospects, each with a familiar tie back to someone *you* know too!

Now let's say that you only end up scheduling appointments with seven of these fifteen people. That's still seven self-generated, more likely to be friendly and willing clients you're about to meet. When you continue with tenacity, making sure your goal is ten referrals on each presentation with a net of five appointments, soon you will have thirty-five new, warm prospects to call. This then turns into eighteen more presentations.

All of a sudden your customer base has mushroomed in two days from three to twenty-eight! Twenty-eight becomes seventy-five, and soon, you're busy with preset appointments weeks in advance, adding new clients and confidence to your arsenal every day. Your persistence is paying off—you're reaching one goal after another and on your way to becoming a millionaire.

Making the Call to the Referral a Friendly One

Another advantage to referrals is that when done properly you can get the referring customer to lay some groundwork for you before you make the call to the new prospect. You could even ask the original customers, whether they've bought anything or not, to call ahead to the people they're referring you to.

If they'll mention that they liked you and that the new prospect might find what you're offering to be of interest, you are likely to quickly have a nicely qualified lead awaiting you. This may sometimes give way to easy, fast sales. Your referred prospect may say things like, "Dave tells me you'll give me a great deal if I like what I see!" A salesperson who never utilizes referrals may go forever without ever hearing that phrase uttered by an excited new prospect.

Why Would They Send You to Their Friends and Relatives?

In the previous section there are two points to notice, which will be the difference between you successfully gaining referrals or not. First, friendliness is a key. If you are anything but likable or present yourself in a way the prospect doesn't feel comfortable with, what are the chances they would ever want to introduce you to a friend or family member?

You're going to be asking prospects for referrals which requires them to dip into their personal or business address books or computer data bases to produce names and phone numbers of people you can potentially see. You may even have asked them to call on your behalf and encourage the person on the other end of the phone to see you. For this whole process to happen, the customer needs to like you.

Second, when asking for referrals, you need to ask for shows, *not* sales. In the previous chapter, when Joe switched his door approach from "Would you like to buy?" to "I get credit for showing," his results were dramatically improved.

You may want to use the fact that you get credit every time you do a presentation when asking for referrals, or in your industry you might offer a free gift or other inducement. But as long as you make it clear that you don't expect the referral to buy anything, your request is less threatening. The truth is you don't care who buys from you and who doesn't. You just want to draw some cards off the deck.

Again, only a friendly salesperson who has been entertaining, polite, courteous, and professional is going to have created an atmosphere in which the customer *wants* to refer friends and family. When you believe in your product, or service, and you are selling something everyone needs to own whether they buy it from you or not, clients or customers will *want* to send you to their friends.

How to Ask for Referrals

When asking for referrals, just like with cold calling, tenacity and an assumptive manner are important. If you meekly ask your customers, "Would you please be nice enough to maybe give me the name of someone who might have a need for my product?" you won't get many names. What you really implied is, "I'm sure the answer to this question is going to be 'no,' but is there by any chance a friend or relative or yours who'd buy something from me?"

Instead, ask confidently as if you expect your customers to produce a wealth of names. Indicate through your attitude and demeanor that, because you have such a great product or service and are such a great salesperson, the customers would be doing a big favor for anyone with whom they put you in contact.

However, your first request may not be successful. You may need to wait a while to when the timing is better. Have a notepad, clipboard, or referral sheet available. This needs to contain names already given to you by previous customers and plenty of blank spaces available for the current prospect to fill in. Just like the piano player who puts the glass jar on top of the piano with a dollar in it, you need to visually prompt your customer to do what you are asking. And always keep in mind that most people are followers so—*you need to be a leader!*

When to Ask for Referrals

Most sales professionals agree that asking for referrals anytime is fine. Some prefer to ask at the beginning of a presentation. They've observed that later after the customer has been asked to buy, he or she may be hesitant to produce any referrals, no matter how nice the salesperson is.

Asking early on, however, could damage the flow of your presentation and may hinder what you're mainly there for, which is to make a sale. Also, if the customer gives you referrals early on, he or she may no longer feel obligated to buy because of the referrals. Since he or she has already given you so many names, his or her attitude may be, "Surely one of the people who I referred you to will buy, so you don't really need me to buy too."

Do what works best for you and the product or service you are selling. Just like with cold calling, the first few times you ask for referrals you may be disappointed in the results. Nonetheless, hang in there and ask every time. If you don't ask, you can virtually be assured your customer will never come to you and say, "Could you run across the street and show it to my neighbor? And when you're done there, my sister would be really interested too, and then...."

The Art of Asking for Referrals

Asking for a referral is simply another approach. A typical referral request might go something like this:

"Mrs. Jones, as you know, I need to show my product five times every day. And I'd much prefer to show it to someone friendly and nice like you whenever I get the chance. It would really help me out if you could jot down ten people you know who would give me an opportunity to meet them and show them what I do. It doesn't matter whether they want to buy anything or not. I'd just like to add them to my client (or customer) list. (The *break* in this approach is handing your referral sheet and pen to the customer). If you'd just jot those down here, I'd really appreciate it."

The first time you ask, you might not receive. The customer may tell you she doesn't *know* ten people. A little prompting may be in order.

"It can be *anybody*, Mrs. Walker—a neighbor, somebody from church, a sister or a relative who lives in town. The only thing I ask is that they're as nice to me as you've been."

Now the customer may produce the names or tell you she doesn't feel comfortable giving out someone's phone number without their permission. That's a natural response, so treat it that way. But you also need to assume this means she has someone in mind.

"Oh, I can understand that Mrs. Walker, but I haven't done anything to offend you in any way today, have I? And of course, you know I'll treat anyone who you refer me to just as professionally as I have you. But, actually, if you *would* call ahead for me to get that permission, I'd prefer that as well. This way you can get the okay from whomever you're thinking of, and maybe you can put in a good word for me. So who do you think would most benefit from seeing what I do?"

If the client or customer mentions one or several people who may be interested, encourage her to call them right now. If she could just let her friends know that a nice friendly man or lady named (you) will be calling this evening to set up a time to show them something, and that it will only take a few minutes.

Now, if the answer is again a no, it might be time to politely proceed with something else and come back to the referral sheet later. But don't put it away. That means you've accepted defeat, and to bring it out again later may seem a little too aggressive and might anger the client. So leave it out and gently come back to it later when you feel the timing is better. Perhaps you can tell that the client doesn't feel comfortable with you yet, or maybe you can think of a better, nonthreatening, softer approach to use.

Sometimes an industrious salesperson will even offer the customer an incentive to provide referrals. This could be done in the form of some small, inexpensive but desirable piece of merchandise from the company, which the prospect would earn by providing "x" number of referrals.

The better you get at sales, the better you'll get at referrals. You may find that while you had to pay for referrals early in your career or business, they come easier and more frequently as you establish confidence and success.

Calling the People on the List of Names

Now that you've got the list of Mrs. Walker's friends and relatives, what do you do with them? The next step involves phone skills, which is covered in Chapter Twelve.

With a referral, though, you still need to stick to the basics of the approach. Remember, your objective is to *show* not sell, and you won't need very much time. Your company gives you credit each time you do a presentation, and you need to do five presentations every day.

Involve these same components when you call a referred prospect. Add some enthusiasm, along with fine-tuning the skills you will learn in the next chapter, and you can benefit from a *better* than 50-percent ratio in setting appointments.

Always remember that people generally want to be around friendly, successful people. They are also more likely to want to refer their family and friends to friendly, successful people. The quicker you start acting as if you are successful, the quicker it can cease to be an act. Know in your heart that you are on your way to becoming a new millionaire, and act that way.

Chapter Eleven

———— $ ————

Telemarketing, Exhibit Marketing, and Draw Boxes

"When you call your prospects,
right away you need to differentiate
yourself from the average or below-average
phone solicitors they've encountered
in the past. Smile."
Brian Gotta

There is a plethora of other methods of lead generation. Some work in one field but may not work in another, depending on the type of product or service you offer and to whom you market them. Some companies enjoy success and get great returns from direct mailing. And some use print and media advertising, even though they are costly and geared more toward retail-oriented businesses. Each method has its place.

Dialing for Dollars

Telemarketing is essential in many sales businesses. Many companies have hourly paid telemarketers who handle the phones and set appointments for their outside salespeople. If you've ever received a call at home or at work from a phone solicitor with a "free offer" from a company, then you have a basic idea of how it works.

Usually you're selected randomly from a list of homeowners, business people, or from the phone book. The telemarketer then reads a scripted pitch that typically ends with a question such as, "Would you like to take advantage of our free offer?" After hearing the obligatory "No thank you," the appointment setter thanks the person for his or her time and dials the next number.

The better telemarketers inject some life into their voices, and the good ones even listen to the prospect, sense small indications of interest, and ask questions. The great ones do all of these things and even attempt to overcome objections. But most hourly paid telemarketers who set appointments for salespeople simply get whatever results they achieve by the sheer volume of calls made. They know that if several hundred people hear the script, sooner or later one or two will be interested in what the particular offer may be.

The main cause of disinterest, even dislike for telemarketers in general, stems from the lackluster delivery given by the average phone representative. Such callers lose sight of the fact that each person who answers the telephone is just that—*a real, live person*, not just another seven- or eleven-digit number.

Chances are you're not looking to be a minimally paid appointment setter. But depending upon the lead generation methods you choose to employ, you'll always have to do at least *some* phone work. You may even work with a commodity that is sold primarily over the phone, with little or no face-to-face contact ever needed. In a sense, you combine the telemarketing and sales venues together in one phone conversation. In any case, understanding the negatives and positives of all the intricacies of telemarketing can help you be even better on the phone.

You may work for a company that may already employ phone solicitors to assist you in getting in front of clients. If so, you're probably paying some or all of the telemarketer's salary by way of weekly contributions to participate in the lead generation program, reduced commissions on telemarketed calls, or some other form of payment. You may have already employed your own telemarketers who get leads only for you. Or you may be in a position where the best or only method of lead generation you can utilize is for you to pick up the phone and set appointments for yourself. Whichever is the case, remember that there are differences between cold calling in person and cold calling over the phone.

When you're in person you can smile and elicit a mirrored smile from the prospect. Face to face, you can use animated body gestures to indicate liveliness, enthusiasm, interest and to make a break in or away. When in person, clients or customers often have a more difficult time saying no to a live, friendly, happy, well-dressed, hard-working professional.

When you are on the phone, however, the prospect doesn't see you—the sparkle in your eye or the smile on your face. The prospect doesn't know if you are sitting in a cubicle or in a spacious office behind a mahogany desk, or if you're dressed to a T or just in a T-shirt. But rest assured, the person on the other end of the phone will probably either not bother to imagine anything, which depersonalizes you, or will imagine the worst. The biggest disadvantage to telemarketing for leads is that it's simply *impersonal*. Therefore, it's rather easy for the prospects to reject and hang up on a faceless, lifeless nonentity whose unsolicited call comes out of the blue.

Let Your Personality Ring Through

When you call your prospects, right away you need to differentiate yourself from the average or below average phone solicitors they've encountered in the past. Smile. They may not be able to see you smile, but they can sure hear it in your voice. If you don't feel much like smiling, and you figure why bother, you're likely to get poor results. Listen to yourself on the phone when you're straight-faced and then when you're smiling. You'll hear the difference and so will your prospects.

Even though your prospects can't see how you're dressed and what a great professional you are, you need to speak up strongly with confidence and vitality in your voice. At least then they can hear it. Just as if you were face to face for the first time, exude confidence, professionalism, happiness, and warmth. Picture what the prospect looks like so you feel more like you *are* talking to a live person face to face.

Get to the Point and Anticipate They May Say No

While there are differences between a telemarketed approach and a personal approach, the majority of the requirements are the same. When on the phone, you will still use most of the same steps as when you're talking face to face.

Introduce yourself quickly and then get right to the point. Tell your prospects immediately why you're calling and what your objective is. Speak with inflection, not in a monotone. Listen to him or her and realize that at first they might not be paying attention to you. Ask a question they don't expect in order to find out if they're listening. As with the door approach, they may be waiting for you to take a breath so they can tell you they're not interested.

If you get an objection from a prospect, pleasantly press on. Agree with your prospect but head back into your approach again, saying the same thing in a different way. Mention that you are only asking for a little time. Help your prospect realize that you're not looking for the sale, rather just to meet and do a presentation, if that's the case. Finally, make the break on the phone. This is done when you book the appointment in an assumptive manner.

I Just Want to Show You What I Do

Allen, who sells life insurance, will demonstrate how he has been so successful cold calling through the phone book and generating leads that turn into sales. His approach is simple, straight to the point, and effective. Here he's calling bank managers in his area.

Allen: "Hi, can I speak to Ken Traynor?"

Ken: "This is Ken."

Allen: "Hi Ken. This is Allen Robertson from Northdale Fidelity. How are you?"

Ken: "Fine."

Allen: "Great. I'm calling because I work with a lot of the Branch Managers in the area, and I'm going to be in your neighborhood on Friday. Is there a time I could stop by to meet you and show you some of the things I do?"

Ken: "I don't think I'll be interested, but thanks anyway."

Allen: "Oh, that's fine. But I'd like to meet you anyway and just drop off my card. Are you going to be in around noon on Friday?"

Ken: "Yeah, but I'm not in the market for anything right now, so I don't want to waste your time."

Allen: "I appreciate that, but I'm going to be right by there anyway on Friday, so I'd like to get a chance to meet you and just leave you my card. Do you mind if I stop by around midday?"

Ken: "I have a lunch meeting at 12:30, and I won't be back until around 2."

Allen: "Okay, good. I'll just stop by around 12 on Friday and look forward to seeing you then.

Ken: "Alright, if you want to."

Allen: "Great. I'll see you Friday at noon. Thanks."

Stick to One Approach

That went pretty smoothly. Let's address all the things Allen did correctly. First, he never deviated from his stated intention, which was just to meet Mr. Robertson. Why? Because if he had mentioned anything on the phone about selling, he never would have set the appointment. Instead, Allen kept coming back to his one harmless and friendly intent, "I just want to meet you and drop off a card." Next, he was persistent. Remember the process: *Objection. Agree. Restate.*

Nowhere in the process do you see the word *Argue,* as in argue with the prospect to overcome the objection. Nor do you see the word *Believe,* as in believe what the prospect is saying, when he or she says, "I'm not interested." Of course he or she isn't interested; you haven't mentioned what you're offering.

Nor does the process include the word *Change,* meaning if the first given reason for your call didn't immediately work, give another reason for the call. If a salesperson shifts from one reason for the appointment to another, and then on to another, the prospect realizes that none of them is the real reason.

The prospect will then determine the *real* reason to be: *He (or she) wants to sell me something.* The prospect is never interested and never has any time or money until you get face to face and present your case. Then, suddenly, everything can change. Time may no longer be an issue. Money might never even come up. Your presentation can create the necessary interest for a yes. So all you want to do is set the appointment. The rest will take care of itself when you meet and make an effective presentation.

Allen, just like a good salesperson who's cold calling, also made an assumptive break. It would be very unlikely he'd ever get an appointment if he just waited for the prospect to book an appointment time for him. By telling the bank manager when he would be there and just getting an okay, Allen made it clear that an appointment time was expected. When the prospect senses you don't expect a yes, it's infinitely easier for him or her to fulfill your expectations and say no.

The Pre-Approach
Another avenue utilized in telemarketing is to make a call as a "warm up" and get permission to send out some literature about the company. The salesperson then mentions that

he or she will give a follow-up call at a later date. This is almost always going to be met with acceptance, because the person being called doesn't feel the need to commit to anything over the phone.

The drawback is that this whole process takes more time. The more steps involved in setting the appointment, the fewer actual presentations are made. Ironically, doing the "warm up" gives the prospect more time to "cool down"! Plus, costs are increased with additional phone time and postage. However, if you are selling a relationship versus a product or service and have time to develop it, this may be the way to go.

Other companies utilize a telemarketing gimmick in order to get themselves in front of prospective clients or customers. This is when the offer is simple and clear: "Witness one of our presentations and we'll give you a free gift." There is nothing tricky about this approach; just make sure you can afford the free gifts and that you do in fact deliver everything you promised on the phone.

Even if you never need to telephone solicit for yourself, phone skills are still critical to your success. There will always be times when you need to speak to your prospects and clients or customers over the phone. You may need to schedule service, reschedule an appointment, ask for clarification, or get an okay on changes to an order. Or you may simply want to call back and make sure everything is satisfactory with the purchase, which, by the way, is an excellent thing to do. Regardless of the reason for your call, confidence, friendliness, and professionalism elevate you from the mire of the ordinary telemarketer into the realm of the people whose persistence, skills, and compassion take them to millionaire status.

Other Ways to Prospect—Exhibit Marketing

Exhibit marketing is when you or your company rent space at a local trade show, home and garden expo, flea market, or something of this sort. Exhibits are easy to find, and the cost of a three-day show, which you could share with associates who join you, might be an affordable way for you to gain advertising. Hundreds of people may walk past your booth every day.

Most of these shows are also great opportunities to close sales, since those prospects usually have some power to purchase and often come to the event planning to buy something. These venues can also be excellent opportunities to generate leads or contacts for follow up later.

Working an exhibit is an art unto itself, and when you have a chance to participate in one, do it. It can be a lot of fun. Exhibit marketing is like a split right down the middle of retail and direct sales, containing some components of both.

Some companies, usually those with small ticket items, use exhibits to display and sell their wares. Other companies, usually those with higher ticket items, use exhibit marketing strictly as an opportunity to advertise and obtain prospects' names to call later. They rarely sell anything on the spot but might create some interest in a prospect and then get a lead to follow up on.

Draw Boxes

If you've ever walked past an exhibit booth or into a business establishment that had a draw box on its counter, then you've witnessed another form of direct marketing. These draw boxes are nothing more than name generators that encourage people to fill out the entry blank provided in hopes they might win the prize.

Once they put their name into the box, it is handled in exactly the same manner as the name from the drawing box at the exhibit. Either an appointment setter or a salesperson contacts the person by phone and books an appointment. If this technique is appropriate for the type of business you're in, then you might want to do it.

What's in a Name?

The most important thing to keep in mind is that every name you receive, through any method of lead generation, is extremely valuable. A prospect who said no today may say yes tomorrow due to a change in his or her circumstances. You can never have too many names and phone numbers.

Make it a priority to amass your own list or database of contacts. Keep careful records and make notations to help you remember the result of each meeting or conversation. When you recall spouse's, children's, and even pet's names, you are that much more likely to be thought of as a friend rather than a salesperson the next time you call.

Discipline yourself to call customers or clients regularly in a friendly and helpful manner. You'll be surprised how often this personal service leads to an "Oh, by the way, I was just telling my friends about you and they're interested in seeing you," referral that you never would have had otherwise.

You're In!

You're finally in front of a prospect! You've completed step one of the three-part process of Get in, Present, and Close. Either through cold calling, referrals, telemarketing, or some other form of lead generation, you get to do your presentation. A prospect has been kind enough or interested enough to let you show your stuff. Get your materials, your product or service, and your facts and figures ready to go! Now that you're in, it's show time!

Chapter Twelve

$

Believe in Your Product, Service, or Opportunity

*"When you believe in your product, service
or opportunity, the presentations you give
will have more credence and be more appealing
to virtually everyone to whom you give them."*
Brian Gotta

Whether you are presenting a tangible or an intangible item, it is essential that your product, service or opportunity be of great value. When you believe what you have to offer is something everyone needs, then you're going to be more convincing and effective in your presentation. If you'd buy it or use it yourself, provided you could afford it, or if you're taking advantage of the opportunity it may present to associate with others and build a business, you'll be more believable

No matter how great what you're sharing is there is still no product, service, or opportunity that sells itself (thank goodness). The minute products, services, and opportunities gain the ability to get in front of a prospect and present themselves, you won't be needed.

But you are needed. You are needed and it all depends on *you*. Your company or supplier needs you or others like you, your family needs you, and *you* need you. Given that you're serious about becoming a millionaire, you need to show your product, service, or opportunity plan multiple times each day (or week, if you're doing it part time, in addition to your day job) so you can prosper and improve your financial picture. What you're offering may be really great. However, it's not something that you can drive around with in your car or sit with in your house and have people run up to you and ask for—making you a millionaire without your diligent effort!

Share What You've Got

As you learn about giving presentations, keep in mind that you can be an expert at getting in front of a prospect, an expert at presenting, and an expert at getting a yes, but if you don't *do* something with those talents and abilities, they're wasted. Also keep in mind that when all is said and done, the marginal salesperson who does many presentations will always outperform the talented one who only does a few.

The real secret is to combine the best of both. Work as hard and as smart as possible while you're honing your skills, and then when you get great at what you do, maintain the strong work ethic you've developed and keep on going.

Question: What do you call a talented salesperson who works hard, smart, and consistently?

Answer: A millionaire in the making.

Say to Yourself, "I Believe!"

One of the best ways to ensure your diligence is to believe so strongly in your product, service, or opportunity that you *want* to share it with everyone. When you feel this way, your attitude says, "If I can just get this in *front* of people, they'll want it!" When you think everyone who sees what you're selling will want it, you naturally want to show it more and more. This leads you to be enthusiastic and believable, both of which make you virtually irresistible. Therefore, you gain sales or associates.

You become even more eager because you get positive reinforcement from your effort as you win at the game of sales. As a result, you gain a greater understanding of your potential and you want to work even harder and smarter. Best of all, while you notice your earnings are growing more and more, you realize you have truly helped some people along the way. That, alone, is gratifying.

Allen from Northdale Mutual has a younger brother Patrick, who also sells for Northdale. Patrick talks about an event that occurred when he was young that stuck with him and ultimately contributed to his going into the life insurance business:

"When I was 16 years old, my brother Allen had just graduated from college and moved out of state. He was starting an insurance sales career. I was a little naïve kid who didn't have a clue yet about the real world.

"One night my brother and his wife were in town visiting. After dinner he was going over to a friend's house where some of his high school and college buddies and their wives were going to gather. I noticed that he was organizing his folders and spread sheets together to take with him. I thought that this seemed tacky and something I would never do. I said, 'You're going to try to sell insurance to your friends?'

"I'll never forget what happened next. He looked at me with a combination of pity and disappointment and said, 'They all *need* it, Patrick.' He believed so strongly in what he was representing that he felt he would be hurting his friends if he *didn't* sell it to them.

"Later on when the time came for me to make my choice in careers, that moment kept coming back to me. I thought 'Why not sell something you'd be proud to sell to your friends and family?' That makes it really easy to sell to everyone else."

So when you believe in your product, service, or opportunity, the presentations you give will have more credence and be more appealing to virtually everyone to whom you give them. And when you develop great, strong work habits, your belief can translate into many sales or recruits mostly by your enthusiastic belief in what you're offering.

But your belief and the willingness to work hard and smart are not enough to sustain you through a long and prosperous sales career or business. The presentation you do is the signature you leave on your work. When you learn the necessary attitude, the techniques used by the sales experts who make a great living in this line of work, and you care about those you serve, you can soon arrive at a point where you feel like you have the best job or business in the world. Maybe you are there already and know that such a conviction is worth the challenges you overcome each day as you strive toward being a millionaire—it is priceless.

When you love and believe in what you do, you never work another day again in your life!

Chapter Thirteen

———§———

The Presentation—Introduction and High Price

*"And though your enthusiasm and caring about
the people you're talking with is key, remember to
always be yourself—a friendly, excited you."*
Brian Gotta

Your presentation is the showcase of all the talent, experience, and training you possess. If you were a baseball player, this would be your at bat. If you were a musician in a symphony, this would be your solo. Because so much of your day and/or evening is probably spent prospecting and traveling, the time you are actually presenting is extremely important to your success.

Many salespeople mistakenly believe that either "getting in" or "closing" are the most important aspects of the sales process. If you were to ask various salespeople which of the three steps they feel least confident in, chances are the response would be split down the middle—half claiming they need to work the most on getting in and the other half need the most help in closing. Almost none of them will answer that the weakest part of their business is their presentation. More times than not, though, the reason these people aren't as successful as they'd like to be is they do ineffective presentations. Here's why....

The Core of Your Presentation

There are several components to doing a great presentation, and each one has several sub-components. When you can effectively do at least half of the steps you've ever learned in a given presentation, you can be very successful. But out of all the parts, two emerge as being the primary ones you need to learn and perform well.

Your objective as you do your presentation is to *build value* and *create need,* which is covered briefly in this chapter and in more detail in the next. When you build the value of what you are presenting *and* create a sense that it is something your prospects really need, then you have done an effective presentation.

You haven't necessarily gotten a yes yet, but you have performed step two—the presentation—to the best of your ability. *Build value and create need.*

A Great Presentation Makes for the Best Closer

If you haven't built the value of what you are offering to a point where the prospect feels it's worth the price you're asking, will they ever buy from you no matter how great you are at closing? Would you buy something you felt was priced higher than it was worth? Of course not.

And if you haven't created the *need* for what you're showing, will a prospect ever buy from you, even if he or she agrees the price is fair? You could rattle off all the pat, standard closes you've ever learned, but if your prospects don't feel they *need* what you're presenting, you probably won't make a sale.

So if you have a challenge with your closing skills, it may lie in what you're doing before you ask the prospect to buy from you. Perhaps if you were to do a more thorough value-building and need-showing presentation, more prospects would *buy* from you instead of you having to *sell* to them. Analyze the presentation you make and ask yourself, "If I knew nothing about what I'm offering and heard the exact same presentation I give, would *I* say yes to it?" It could very well be that you have a challenge presenting rather than in the closing itself.

An Effective Presentation Can Spur Motivation

How about the sales professionals who claim they can't get in front of enough prospects and that step one of the sales process is their weakness? How might their presentation be at the root of their problem as well? If they aren't ever in front of anyone, what difference does it make how ineffective their presentation may be?

Here's the answer: In order to get in front of prospects, you need to *seriously want to be in front of them.* If your presentation is weak, resulting in few if any prospects ever getting in the mood to purchase from or associate with you, the number of people you need to see in order to get a yes will be much too high. If you don't see any likelihood of getting a yes once you're in front of someone, if your sales-to-presentation ratio is one out of twenty, are you really earnest in your desire to get out and prospect? Or are you just fooling yourself that you want to prospect?

Who would ever want to go through the challenges of weeding out all the noes it may take just to get a presentation, so that in all probability they could do a lot more work in the presentation only to be told no again? Is there any reason for anyone to go through all that effort and then not be paid any money for it?

But when you do a topnotch presentation that causes your prospects to not only want what you are offering, but also to feel they *need* it, then all the prospecting *is worth it!* You just can't wait to go out and do your presentation again and again. You become unstoppable on the phone or face to face because you know that by getting in front of the prospect you have a 25 percent to 50 percent chance of getting a yes. All of this fervor and ability starts with being able to master the easiest part of the three-step process: the presentation.

You may have been taught to do your presentation from a scripted, verbatim "pitch." Or you may be marketing a new product or service with few or no guidelines and be somewhat "flying by the seat of your pants" in your marketing efforts.

The ideal situation is found somewhere in the middle of these two scenarios: to be able to learn some basic, fundamental steps—some proven and tested methods of presentation—and then adjust them to fit your own personality. This eliminates the delivery of a stale, canned, robotic product demonstration or opportunity presentation, and leaves you with a framework to rely on. And though your enthusiasm and caring about the people you're talking with is key, remember to always be yourself—a friendly and excited you.

Four Presentation Laws of Success and Two Essentials

Law Number One is: *"Don't prejudge the prospect."* While experience will help you learn which prospects are more qualified than others, it is quite possible you may *never* get to a point where you absolutely know who will say yes and who won't, without going through all of the steps of your presentation. If you encounter early objections or perceived unfriendliness, these may just be the prospect's way of fighting off his or her own early urges to say yes. Don't take these things to heart. Use them as encouragement—*not* discouragement.

There are several more laws to be aware of, which will come later. You can learn them slowly, gaining your knowledge as you gain experience, or you can learn them quickly by reading more about the essentials of a great presentation.

Whatever you are presenting, there are always a couple of basic essentials to follow. Essential Number One is: Briefly Introduce Yourself and the Company You Work With, or Your Own Independent Business. This can help to establish you as a solid member of a solid organization, laying the foundation for trust. Mentioning a little history of your company or business and educating the prospect on the advantages your company or business offers may also be helpful.

This also leads to <u>Law Number Two of the presentation:</u> <u>*"Don't overeducate."*</u> "Actions speak louder than words," as the old saying goes. Don't bore your prospects with rote specifications and other details of your product, service, and/or opportunity. Some prospects will want more details and may ask you for them. If you reel off a seemingly endless and monotonous stream of statistics and facts, your prospects are likely to quickly regret letting you start your "speech." They will, in all probability, go from having some level of interest and comprehension to figuring out an alternate game plan. They won't be thinking about what you're saying anymore, but rather what polite emergency they can concoct to get rid of you.

If all it took to make a sale were a series of facts and information, you wouldn't be needed. A brochure would serve the same function, and no one has to pay it any commission or bonuses! The difference between a flyer and a professional, dynamic presentation is *you*! Watch yourself, listen to yourself, and pay attention to your prospect. (Hopefully you can tell if you're boring someone.) Would *you* be interested in what you are saying during your presentation? Or would you be yawning too? If so, maybe less on the education and more action is in order.

This leads to <u>Law Number Three:</u> <u>*"Involve your prospect."*</u> Regardless of what you're presenting, always ask your prospect a lot of questions about his or her needs and wants relevant to what you've got to offer. And be complimentary. Now that you're in front of your prospect, you want to be given a chance, not told that the time is up and ushered to the door.

There is an easy way to make sure you're given the time you need to make your presentation. Here's a hint: What do people like to talk about the most? You and your wonderful product, service, or opportunity?

No! *People like to talk about themselves.* When is the last time you told your prospects they have a beautiful home or office, great looking children, a nice car, or a sharp tie? (Be careful. Don't stray from sincere compliments to transparent, fawning flattery). Upon hearing these kind remarks, do you think the prospect would rather get rid of you or maybe keep you around a little longer?

When you can assist in building your clients' or customers' self-esteem, while being sincerely interested in them and what they're telling you, chances are they'll be glad they let you present. Don't gush, but act as if you were invited to dinner to meet your future in-laws. It's time to sell your best self !

Many salespeople omit a good introduction. They're so excited to be able to do a presentation that they only see the prospect as a giant wallet waiting to be emptied. Most ineffective salespeople never give themselves a chance when doing a presentation because they forget the human element of what they're doing. These salespeople are focused only on themselves and what they can gain, rather than being honestly interested in the real live person in front of them—and wanting to serve that person with what they have to offer.

This brings up Law Number Four: *"Don't sell too early."* Jumping too quickly into the sales mode is an instant turnoff. Plus, since you get paid handsomely every time you sell your product or service, don't you think a little work needs to precede that payday? An effective presentation is a series of balancing acts. Compliment without insincerely flattering. Educate without boring the client or customer. Be friendly while maintaining your professionalism. Get down to business but don't sell too soon. Take your time and be patient, but be careful you maintain a reasonable pace so the client or customer is less likely to feel you are infringing upon their valuable time.

As you become an expert, you'll learn to perform all of these functions simultaneously. You will find closing much less challenging, and have even less of a challenge getting in front of people to do your presentation. You will love getting up and prospecting in the morning (or prospecting on your off time if you still have a full-time job or another business). It will show in your presentation and in your growing income.

Throw Out a High Price

Many salespeople, especially those selling a high-ticket item, are afraid of mentioning their product's price. Since either they presently cannot afford it themselves, or they have yet to gain total confidence in their product and its worth, they're scared to tell their prospects how much it costs. This leads to a big challenge later on in the close.

Chances are while the presentation is going on, the prospect is wondering how much the product costs. Unless you mention the cost, he or she usually estimates the price to be much lower than it actually is. You can then imagine their reaction when a salesperson, who already lacks confidence, finally gets the courage to mention the price, and it's two or three times higher than the prospect had figured on.

Prospect (upon hearing price): "Oh! That's way too much!"

Salesperson (packing up to leave): "Yes, here's my card. Call me if you win the lottery."

You need to set up the prospect's expectations of the price early on in your presentation. You can do this in a variety of ways. One approach is found in <u>Essential Number Two: Throw Out a High Price</u>. Begin your presentation by producing a prewritten contract with your highest package price totaled and taxed at the bottom. You probably don't expect anyone to buy at this price, although if someone did, he or she would get everything indicated. This gives you a starting price to absorb some of the inevitable "sticker shock."

Another method you may choose is to verbally mention a price that's higher than what you hope to get. This can be accomplished by saying, "I can tell you think this is probably worth _____ " (give a price well above the actual sales price of your product).

Or you may want to say, "As great as this is I can't believe the monthly payments are only _____ " (again, something way up there). Or when the prospect shows early in the presentation that he or she is impressed with some aspect of your product, you could say, "That's why we get _____ (four or five times the actual price) for each one."

All of these comments, if said with a smile, open up several doors to you, but in a nonthreatening way. Otherwise you spend all of your time doing an excellent presentation while simultaneously dreading the moment you need to reveal the price.

Before your prospects have the inclination to ask about the price, you let them know what you're selling is expensive. By your confident, carefree manner of conveying that information, you communicate that you think your product is a great value. Next, by throwing out a higher price, you set your prospects up for hearing the *actual* price and thinking it's a bargain. If your prospect battles between loving and wanting your product and not wanting to pay the exorbitant price you first mentioned, they will probably jump at any lower price. And, equally important, by giving out a price early, you say to your prospects, "This product is for sale, and I expect you to want it."

A Salesperson in Action

Paul is in charge of a team of salespeople who represent high-end, commercial-grade blenders. He uses a clever analogy to explain to his salespeople how important it is to raise the prospects' expectation of the price.

"The blenders we sell are more than just blenders. They have several different functions and they're extremely durable. In fact, they have a warranty that is five times longer than the life span of most run-of-the-mill department store blenders. But they sell for nearly five hundred dollars, and I think that's a bargain. Most people, however, perceive a blender to be something they can buy anywhere for $39.95.

"I discovered that my reps could make a great product presentation, but they were saving the price for the end. So all of the prospects who were watching this presentation and falling in love with the product were telling themselves, 'I'll bet that's one of those fancy eighty-nine-dollar blenders. It might even be a hundred!' When they learn that the product actually costs five times that, it blows them out of the water.

"One time I got my sales force together to address this problem. I asked two of our reps how much they thought the new top of the line Mercedes cost. One of them said $50,000, while the other guessed $75,000. You should have seen their faces blanch when I told them it was $135,000.

"I then asked them, 'Imagine you came into some money, and you decided you were going to buy the top of the line Mercedes. You walk into the dealer expecting it to be $60,000 to $75,000 and you go for a test drive. The whole time you're driving it, the salesperson is afraid of the price and doesn't mention it. When you get back to the dealership, the salesperson brings out a contract that reads $135,000 plus tax and licensing. What's your reaction going to be?' After the heart attack you nearly have, you decide you'll buy a house, not a car.

"Now let's say you go in, but this time the salesperson is a little smarter. While you're driving it he says, 'Nice Mercedes, isn't it?'

"You respond confidently, 'Sure is. I think I'm going to get it.'

"And he says (even more confidently), 'That's why we get $250,000 for it! We call it the dollar-a-mile program. Of course, you'll probably get more than 250 thousand miles out of it.'

"At this point you want to just pull over and let him take the car back in. You're gripping the wheel so tightly he has to ask you not to dent the leather. When you get back to the dealership, he coaxes you to come in and sit down, even though you're telling him to forget it.

"'Just look at this,' he says with a smile. And he hands you a contract for $135,000. Now what's your reaction going to be? You'd most likely say, 'Oh, that's more like it. That's what I thought they ran!'

"But that's *not* what you thought they ran half an hour ago. You thought they were $60,000. But by raising your expectation of the price beyond what it actually was, the salesperson made $135,000 look like a bargain.

"My salespeople all got the message," Paul continues. "Now at the beginning of every presentation they mention that the customer might have seen this blender for eight or nine hundred dollars elsewhere. And since at this point in the demonstration none of the prospects want to buy anyway, this doesn't even cause a ripple. But it sets the stage for later, when the customer is thinking, 'Boy, I'd still love to have that blender, but I'm not paying eight or nine hundred dollars for it.'

"When they hear that it sells for only $479.95, and that today's special is fifty dollars off of that, they think it's a great deal. It's not uncommon for customers to ask us how much extra all the attachments we've shown them will run. When they hear that for that one low price they get everything we showed them and more, a lot of times they buy another one for a gift. We found that just the simple step of mentioning a higher price at the beginning of our demo led to an incredible increase in sales."

Here's another example. Have you ever watched a television commercial selling a product you could purchase by calling a toll free number? Next time you see one, pay particular attention at the end to how they give you the price. Unless it's a $20 item, chances are they'll tell you something such as "You'd expect this to sell for as much as $149! But with this special offer, you won't pay $149. You won't even pay $129! You can own this for one easy payment of only $79.95! That's right, only $79.95!"

Why do you think the people selling the product get the price out that way? Because it works. By the time the consumer hears all of the higher amounts, whatever price the commercial finally lands on sounds like a giveaway.

The Good News Is...

If you understand people, you'll understand the philosophy behind giving the price. No matter what, almost without exception, the first price anyone hears is going to be too much. So if the first price you mention is your rock bottom price, you're nearly always going to be disappointed. Whatever product or service you offer, make sure you're not hiding from the cost. When you get a few minutes into the presentation and have established some rapport, smile and mention that a product or service this great is obviously worth _____ (an amount much greater than it sells for).

Don't worry about your prospects reaction to this. In fact, have fun with it. They're not going to throw you out. They don't plan on buying anything at this stage yet anyway. You haven't even begun to build value or create need yet, so what do they care if it's expensive?

But as you proceed to get them interested, to show them how they actually need what you're offering, you have a great inner confidence knowing they think the product or service is more expensive than it is. Rather than dreading the price, you can't wait to reveal it to them. If they ask you "Is it really that much?" You can even tantalize them a little by saying, "It should be, for all it does." Never have you actually come out and told them a false price, but by leading them to believe the investment to be greater than it is, you accomplish a great deal.

When you learn the psychology behind this step, you are a more effective negotiator in all aspects of business and in life. Always remember that when you need to give people some good news and some bad news, *always give the bad news first*. After the initial shock of the bad news hits (in this case the price), the offsetting good news (in the above example the combination of the quality of the product and the actual, lower price) cushions the blow and perhaps even compensates for it.

Figure out what works for you in your situation and have some fun with it, but learn to be confident about your product or service and its price. Good things never come cheap, and if you effectively build value and create need, a prospect will pay almost anything for what you have to offer.

Chapter Fourteen

———$———

The Presentation—More About Building Value and Creating Need as Well as Mini-Closes

"Simply put, when your prospect believes he needs your product or service, that's what makes it valuable."
Brian Gotta

Although building value and creating need are two different and separate components, they're still intertwined. When you build value, it lends itself to creating need, which then enhances a product's or service's value. Simply put, when your prospect believes he needs your product or service, that's what makes it valuable.

Two More Essentials and Another Law of the Presentation

Essential Number Three is: Build Value and Create Need. So what's the difference between building value and creating need? In a nutshell, a product's or service's value can be found in various ways. It may be easier to use, more labor saving, aesthetically more appealing, handier to store, have more features, is faster, more powerful, more convenient and efficient, or will depreciate at a lesser rate than the product or service it is replacing. Perhaps the product's warranty or company's service may be superior to others. A product or service is *valuable* because it has the features and benefits that the customer wants.

A product or service is *needed*, however, when it saves time or money, offers peace of mind, health, security, or will in some way pay for itself many times over after the initial investment. Of the two, which aspect is more important—building value or creating need?

The Only Car With Brakes

Think of the answer to that question this way: If you could have any car you've ever seen on the road what would it be? Most people think of an expensive, prestigious vehicle of some kind. For the sake of this example, let's say it's a new Cadillac. Now if you put that Cadillac next to a less expensive car you may currently own, you'd have no problem being convinced that the Cadillac is more valuable, right? But do you *need* the Cadillac?

No! The car you have now is probably dependable and takes you where you want to go. So even though the Cadillac is clearly more valuable, it's not a necessity. Therefore, until you have some *expendable* income, it's likely you won't buy yourself a new Cadillac.

Now imagine that the Cadillac was the only vehicle on the market that had brakes. One day you think to yourself, "I am tired of slamming my car into a tree every time I want to stop it, paying the body shop to fix the front end, and then crashing into the garage again when I get home." You may start thinking about spending the extra money on the Cadillac. Why? Because when you realize you'll soon spend more money on body repairs for your current car than the cost of the Cadillac, you realize you *need* the Cadillac.

This is the difference between value and need. If you could only show one or the other to a prospect, the need would always win. This is where so many salespeople fall off track. Instead of believing their job or business is to find and then fulfill their prospects' needs, they think that by performing a slick, polished presentation full of features and benefits, their prospects will automatically know they need it.

If you don't *create* need, your prospects regard your product or service as a luxury. They may put it on their wish list, wistfully decline your best offer and then say, "Sure, when I win the lottery." Why? Because at no time did your prospects ever think they *needed* the product. Therefore, they put it way down on their priority list, behind all the things they really *do* need. It's up to you to make what you're offering something people will buy, even if they *don't* have any expendable income.

Create Your Own Success

Your ability to create need is what sets you apart from marginally paid sales clerks in other sales venues. In order for a sale to be made in any type of retail situation, a customer must first walk into the store and already be in need of a product. A good retail employee or business owner might up-sell or add on, but without that customer being lured into the store to begin with, the retail salesperson has a zero chance of making a sale.

How do these customers generally get drawn into retail locations? Through advertising. The department store owners spend millions of dollars on print, radio, and television advertising. They rent enormous, expensive storefronts and place big advertisements in the phone book. Where does the money come from for all that overhead?

The clerks who work in the stores and earn little or no commission when they ring up an item pay the overhead. Since the need for their product was already provided for them and the creation of that need had a tremendous cost, their earnings potential is low and always will be.

Knowing that, you can be patient with yourself when you don't always succeed in sales. Wishing for the "stability" and "security" of the hourly or weekly income that retail employees earn is fruitless. Obviously, that isn't the way to get rich.

You are a creative salesperson. This is why you're paid so well. You *create* a need where there was none before. You find a prospect who otherwise never would have sought out you or your company or business. Every time you gain a sale, you also gain a customer who, in all likelihood, never would have been a customer if it weren't for you. You, not a television commercial, newspaper ad, or huge billboard, brought that person in. Who gets the money that otherwise would have been paid to the television station or the newspaper? You do!

It's probably clear to you now that there are differences between building value and creating need. *You* know them, but do your prospects? Your job is to educate them as to not only why your products or services are superior to the competition (value), but also *why they need them.*

Luxury Doesn't Sell

Joe, our Schilling Windows salesman, inadvertently learned a valuable lesson about need from his father-in-law, Lee.

"I had been selling windows for about nine months and was at my father-in-law's house for Christmas," reveals Joe. "I was in the midst of having a bad (low sales) December and couldn't figure out why. My prospects claimed they couldn't afford anything because of the holidays, and I believed that a little. But some of the reps in my office were having their best month of the year, even though I knew they were hearing the "holiday objection" just as much as I was. I couldn't pinpoint why I wasn't selling like I used to.

"Lee didn't know much about my product because he lived in another area of the country and I had never shown him what I did. He just figured people bought them because of all the good things my wife said about the windows. She told him how much easier they were to get up and down, how easy they were to clean, and all of the other nice features. He'd been in sales all his life, and while we were talking he mentioned to me that he really admired what I did because I sold a 'luxury' item.

"I'll never forget when he said that, because the luxury aspects of my product are strictly secondary. Almost no one buys them because they are prettier, easier to get up and down, or easy to clean. They buy them because they'll provide hundreds and thousands of dollars in energy-cost savings over the life of the home, due to their insulating and sealing qualities. They also offer a better quality of life because of their noise reduction. All the other features are simply a bonus.

"While *I* knew that my windows weren't a luxury item, my father-in-law's comment taught me that my customers may consider them to be nothing more than a luxury. And they were going to continue thinking that unless I educated them. And lately, that was the part of my presentation I was missing.

"I was doing a flashy features-oriented demonstration with my samples, showing a customer all of the attractive but cosmetic advantages to my product. I had gotten away from what had made me so successful when I started, which was my ability to explain how the windows were going to save the customer money.

"Once I got back to the basic premise of my presentation, I started selling again. I went back rejuvenated and had a great January. And I credit much of that success to my father-in-law."

Do You Need a Haircut?

When you learn to build value and create need you're on your way to doing a great presentation, right? Well, yes and no. Each of these parts is extremely important, but value and need alone do not get you a sale. Building value and creating need simply gets the prospect to like the product and want it. You still need to get him or her in the mood to buy.

It's like a haircut. You may look in the mirror and say to yourself, "I need a haircut." But does that mean you'll actually run right out and get one today? Probably not. In fact, you may tell yourself "I need a haircut" for a week or two before you finally take the time to do it. Fortunately for barbers and hairstylists, your hair keeps growing. So even if you procrastinate, your hair will eventually get so long you can't stand it anymore and you'll get it cut.

Unfortunately for you, though, your prospects' needs don't usually keep growing after you make your presentation. They may tell you "I need it," but unless you get them to do something about it, chances are you'll never get their business. After you leave, all the emotion is gone. All your samples, statistics, charisma, charm, urgency, and reasons to buy are gone. Your prospects are then left with two things: a price and your phone number.

Once you've left, your product or service has been pushed way down on the priority list. They've got other things they need more. They got along fine without it before you showed up, didn't they? You arrived and created the need out of thin air. When you leave, that need often leaves with you.

You need to learn approaches that provide your prospects with the proper incentives and motivation to buy from you while you present your product or service. The time to actually ask for the order and truly close the sale will come later. First you'll need to set the stage for the close throughout your presentation.

When you are demonstrating or presenting your product, service or opportunity, everything you say and do is important. Showing is always better than telling, and some products or services lend themselves to a visual demonstration better than others. This brings up Essential Number Four: Mini-Closes. Regardless of what you are presenting, the small mini-closes you make along the way help determine whether or not you're even in the ball game when the end of your presentation comes. The ability to set up the prospect for a close is as important as the ability to close itself.

A little earlier we discussed that when you leave a prospect, so does all of the emotion, value, need, and so forth. Think of it like this: as soon as you begin your presentation, it's as if you have put a pan of water on the stove with the burner on high.

In this analogy, the optimum time to make the sale is when the water is boiling. If you shortcut and sell too early, the water may be warm but not hot enough. Conversely, if you wait too long to ask for the sale, the water has boiled out of the pan. You need to look at the water, and when it boils, close the sale. However, there's one catch. The stove and the pan are just a little too high up to see. So if you can't actually look at it, how do you know if the water is boiling or not?

You use mini-closes. A mini-close serves several functions, but mainly it's a temperature tester. Each mini-close is like you reaching up and touching the water in the pan to see if it's hot. The more mini-closes you use in your presentation, the better gauge you will have of your prospect's temperature, and the better timing you will have when you ask for the sale.

The Umpire

Have you ever heard the old adage about umpires in baseball? The question goes, "At the end of the game, how do you know if the umpires did a good job?" The answer is "If you didn't even notice they were there."

Not remembering an umpire at game's end is the highest compliment he or she can attain. It means the umpire quietly did his job, let the players decide the game, and didn't cause any interruptions in its flow.

A great salesperson is identical to a great umpire. With the use of subtle mini-closes during your presentation, you not only aid the flow of your presentation, but you also help your prospects feel as if they're participants. Instead of feeling like combatants having to fend you off at every turn, your prospects feel as if they are sharing a common purpose with you!

When you become adept at this technique, you'll no longer seem like a "salesperson"; rather, you'll be more like an advisor, even a friend. Most importantly, your customers won't feel like they've been sold something; instead, they'll feel as if they arrived at their own decision without any pressure, and of their own freewill.

The Mini-Close in Action

Here's how it works. A mini-close can be an assumptive statement. It can be an innocent question. It can be in an "if... then" form or alternative question. A mini-close may be as subtle as a choice of pronoun. Some will combine many facets together. The more of them you utilize and the more subtle they are, the stronger your presentation.

While you're doing a presentation, you're engaging the person in conversation and explaining your wares. You have a product or service and some information about it to give your prospects. The goal is that they make a well-informed decision to buy. *The manner in which you provide this information is the key to your success.*

Let's suppose you are selling copiers. You're in front of a prospect who already has a copier, and your challenge is to help the prospect realize that he needs to replace his old machine with the new one you're selling. A strong selling point of your product is that it's extremely fast, and therefore saves time. How are you going to get that point across? The first and least effective way would be like this:

"Mr. Davis, when you want to make multiple copies with your current copier, you have to place your document under the tray here and then hit the keypad. It usually takes a couple of minutes to warm up. Then you have to wait a long time for your copies to come out one by one. But with my machine, all you'd do is put the document on top here, hit this button for the number of copies, and you're done twice as fast. Nothing could be easier or faster."

That didn't sound so bad. What was wrong with that approach to showing a feature? Let's compare it to better way to show it.

"Mr. Davis, when you want to run multiple copies of a document with this Relica, what do you have to do? Do you have to lift this tray here, place the document underneath, and then hit the keypad? Does it take a couple of minutes to warm up? Do you then you have to wait a long time for your copies? It's a long process isn't it? Do you think it'll be any easier from now on with the Mercurica, if all you have to do is pop the document right here on top, hit the number of copies you need, then let it run? And if it gets them done twice as fast, do you think that will have saved you some time?"

What was the difference? In both scenarios, essentially the exact same information was given. The difference was in the delivery. In the first case, everything was stated as fact. The information was *told* to the customer, forced upon him, and was not open for discussion. No matter how friendly and affable the salesperson might be, the message was "These are facts about my product that you *must* believe." No one likes to be *sold* anything, but to perform your presentation in this manner puts your prospect in that unenviable position of someone who is being *sold* to.

So what happened the second time? Even though the same points were brought out, they were done in the form of seemingly non-leading questions. Twelve questions were asked so that the prospect didn't feel as if he were being forced to believe a series of facts given him by an obviously biased salesperson.

Rather, the prospect was simply answering a string of innocent questions to provide more information to his "impartial advisor." The entire tone was different, yet the same facts were conveyed.

Next, what *kind* of questions were those twelve? Each of them elicited a yes response. Throughout the entire conveyance of that feature, the prospect was nodding his head saying, "Yes, yes, yes...."

If your prospect says yes each time you show a feature during your presentation, is that a positive or negative for what you're endeavoring to accomplish? If throughout your entire presentation the customer is willingly responding yes, yes, yes, yes, is it less or more likely he will continue to say yes when you ask him to buy?

One Word Can Make a Difference

Did you notice any other differences? In the first, less effective scenario the Mercurica salesperson referred to the prospect's current equipment (the Relica) as *"your copier,"* and to the Mercurica as *"my machine."* In the second case he referred to them correctly as "the Relica" and "the Mercurica." Later on he might even refer to the two of them as "the old machine" and "the new Mercurica."

This may seem like a minor point, but everything you say to a prospect adds up and factors into the decision. If you refer to the old product often enough as "his" and the new one as "yours," that's how they are going to remain when the presentation is complete—"his and yours." *By taking ownership away from both machines, you've subtly dispossessed him of one and freed him to claim possession of the other.*

What else happened? Did you notice the assumptive statement made in the second delivery? The first time the salesperson said, "But with my machine all you'd do is place the document..." Compare that to the second presentation when the salesperson asked, "Do you think it'll be any easier from now on with the Mercurica if all you have to do is pop the document right here on top...?"

What could be more subtle, assumptive, and effective than that second statement? In lieu of using "you'd," which translates to "you would" as in "you would, maybe, perhaps, *if* you ever bought," he said "it'll," meaning "it will, definitely." Then he threw in "from now on," again implying "You already own this product, I'm *assuming* you will buy."

Also, when referring to the Relica, the salesperson simply "placed" the document underneath the tray, whereas when describing the Mercurica, the salesperson had the ability to "pop" whatever needed to be copied right on top. Use active words when referring to your product or service and passive words when referring to the competition.

By now you may feel as if you've been through psychology class. But choosing your words carefully increases your success. It's easy to adjust your words from ones that convey "I hope you'll buy" to ones of assumed ownership and possession. For example, "This is *your* owner's manual that comes with it," compared to "This is *the* owner's manual that comes with it." It's also just as easy to speak in present tense as it is to use words that convey future, or "if." For example, "From now on this is how you'll be able to..." compared to "By purchasing this you could..."

And it's just as easy to phrase your facts in the form of a question as it is to state them authoritatively. For example, "Do you think it'll be any easier from now on if...?" compared to "This is the easiest way to do this on the market. You'll love it."

None of these small changes is so blatant that any prospect will even pick up on them. No one prospect is going to say, "Hey! You said 'It *will* be easier from now on,' not 'It *would* be easier!' Don't assume I'm going to buy!"

But throughout the course of a presentation, your carefully chosen words have a collective, positive impact, and they help you gauge where you are in your presentation. If one of these probes is met with, "Yes, that *will* be easier," you just learned that the water is almost boiling, and you wouldn't have known that without asking the question.

Tie Down Closes

These techniques are referred to as mini-closes because they lay the foundation for the final close later. Another often used euphemism is "tie-down close." These small phrases act in concert to bring your prospect step by step closer to your desired objective.

For example, if you're selling pots and pans, you may say, "Where will you store these? In the cupboard or under the stove?" If you're selling home-security systems, you may say, "Will you need the keypad on the left side of the door or the right?"

Utilize questions that elicit answers you want. "Would you use this if you had it?" is a great tie down question. These seem to the untrained mind like harmless, fact-finding questions, but they are in fact little tie downs and little temperature tests.

Do you want to be the umpire who goes through the game conspicuously or unnoticed? Do you want to be the salesperson who seems pushy, aggressive, and even obnoxious, or do you want to be a helpful part of a smooth process while masterfully guiding your prospects toward your objective? Your ability to direct your prospects will determine which one you'll be.

If you're blunt and forceful, your prospects will always have the feeling they're being sold to, and they'll naturally resist. But if you use some tact, relay your facts and information in the form of innocuous questions, subtly engage the person in this manner, and add some light humor, then he or she is likely to feel much more at ease about the decision and less hesitant to make it.

What it all boils down to is that most people have been taught not to believe salespeople. But no one will reject something *shown* to them ("Believe your eyes, not your ears"). Couple this with the masterful step of asking questions that let the prospects feel like their making up their own mind, and you are in the enviable position of having prospects *come to you*, instead of needing to run after them.

All this leads to Law Number Five: *"Listen to the prospect."*

Shhh! Did you Hear That?

Not everything the prospect says to you will be so blatant as "Yes! I'll take it!" or "Can I write you a check?" In fact, you may go six months of working hard without ever hearing those precise words. However, train your ears to *listen* to what he or she is saying, and before long you'll realize that many of the things a prospect says are just as clearly an indication of being ready to buy, though not articulated in so many words.

What you need to listen for are buying signs, indications of interest, examples of needs you can fulfill, and clues that indicate you may be close to a sale. Most of the time you'll need to read between the lines and realize that prospects often say the *opposite* of what they mean.

Here are some examples of what trained listening means. A rookie salesperson is doing a presentation. As the presentation begins, the prospect says to the newcomer warningly, "I'm not buying anything today."

The new salesperson gets immediately deflated. She thought everything was going so well and that maybe this time she had something. Now, the minute she gets a little excited, the prospect tells her he's not buying today. Unfortunately, the salesperson believes it. This is a case where she heard but didn't listen.

Think about it. Why do you think the prospect felt the need to tell the salesperson he wasn't buying? *Because he was already fighting the urge to buy, and he said it more to discourage himself than to discourage her!*

Unfortunately, the untrained salesperson hears this and figures it's a true statement. She mentally quits on this presentation.

A trained salesperson, on the other hand, listens and even agrees, saying, "Oh, I know you're not going to buy. Now let me show you this." The trained salesperson thinks to him or herself, "I've got one!" He or she knows the prospect *really* means, "I'm afraid I'm ready to buy something. You better not do your job well."

Trained listening is also a matter of sometimes letting the prospects talk about themselves. After a little prompting, you can get most people to open up and tell you a lot about their lives, and this benefits you in several ways. For example, if you're in a prospect's office and you notice pictures of his children on the desk, you can compliment his fine looking family. He'll likely accept the compliment and thank you.

But delve a little deeper. Ask him how old they are. When he says, "This one is five, this one is three, and the baby just turned one," you've given him the opening to elaborate. He may tell you their names if you ask. Ask him if the older one is in school yet or if any of them play any sports. Ask him something to encourage him to open up. When you push the right buttons, sit back and listen. The more he expands upon his personal life, the better it is for you.

Keep Them Talking

Listen to your prospects carefully. When you sense they may be finishing it up, think of another question to keep them going on the subject. Do your best to make sure they elaborate as much as possible. You'll be glad they did.

Your prospects will give you clues about how you can sell them better. They are also going to appreciate your genuinely caring nature. Anyone who opens up to us sees us more as a friend, causing some of the walls between salesperson and prospect to come down. This is what creates the atmosphere for your prospects to be more trusting of you!

After your prospects have taken up a nice chunk of your time telling you all about their life, they usually feel more obligated to you. The realization hits that "Gee, I've hogged so much of this person's time talking about all of this personal stuff. I'd better listen to what she has to say." Your prospects may even become a little sheepish upon realizing they've been bragging and may apologize and encourage you to begin your presentation.

Your response then could be, "Not at all. I really enjoyed it, but I know you're busy too. Now here's what we have." The transition is seamless. Your prospects then give you the floor and want to accommodate you in any way. They now trust you more, sense you're a nice person, and will listen to you just as attentively as you listened to them.

Is Three Years Old Too Young?

Trained listening also involves attempting to size up your prospect as best you can, and then adjusting your presentation to fit. Todd is a district manager for a company specializing in Time Share property sales. He shares a story of being at an exhibit show where he discovered one of his salespeople had a listening challenge.

"We were at a show and one of my brightest new reps, Mike, was talking to a young lady. She couldn't have been more than thirty years old. Our average customers are couples in their fifties or sixties who want a little vacation spot a few times a year. And they usually like the fact that their kids can use the place once in a while. Plus it makes a great gift to send their kids on a vacation whenever they want. We sell that feature of our product all the time.

"Mike had been using this close all day, and when he spoke with this nice young lady, I was surprised to hear him use the same close on her. He told her, 'You can have your kids use the condo whenever. They'll have a nice vacation place.'

"He was simply saying the words, not really meaning them, and he wasn't even looking at her. He was looking at the paperwork and writing. She was very polite and didn't say anything back. She just let him proceed.

"Then Mike said it again. 'It's great to be able to have a place you can send your son or daughter.' This time the lady was a little embarrassed and said quietly, 'Well, my daughter is only three,' but Mike wasn't listening. He kept right on going with what he was saying. Mike was such a hard worker and a bright young man, but he had gotten in the habit of saying, saying, saying. He relied on overpowering customers instead of listening, helping and using finesse."

"Red Light" Questions

A trained listener learns to hear buying signs. Questions such as "How much is it?" "What's the warranty?" "What does it come with?" "My old product won't do this, does yours do that?" and "Do you finance?" are examples of *Red Light Questions*. Whenever you hear one of those questions, a red light needs to come on in your head telling you, "I've got one here! This person is already thinking about buying."

Whenever you hear a question such as, "What's the warranty?" you need to ask yourself, "Why would he want to know that if he wasn't thinking about buying?" Sometimes a prospect may even combine a red light question with a negative positive statement, which should really get you excited. She may say, "I'm not buying anything, but just out of curiosity, how much is it?" In this situation the prospect is interested while fighting that interest at the same time!

Your use of mini-closes is certainly enhanced by listening carefully. Listening opens the door to opportunities to use these tie downs. The most effective and useful tie down closes you can utilize are "if...then" closes. The more "if...then" phrases and questions you employ, the stronger your presentation. Here is an example of combining listening with a tie down close to bring the person one notch closer to the sale.

Prospect: "Does it have a warranty?"

Salesperson: "*If* it had a great warranty, *then* would that be important to you?"
or
Prospect: "What does that come with?"
Salesperson: "*If* it came with everything I've shown you, *then* you'd want it, right?"

Not every question needs to actually contain the words "if" and "then" to have the same meaning. For instance, "Would you use this if you had it?" is just as powerful as any "if...then" and elicits the proper, positive response.

Use Your Eyes

Some time during the course of your sales career or business, someone will tell you an old adage about listening: "You've got two ears and only one mouth." That means you need to listen twice as much as you talk, which is excellent advice.

Did you also notice that you have two eyes as well? Trained listening also involves your observations of the prospect's demeanor. When the prospect is talking, what are his or her mannerisms? Does he or she look attentive and alert? Is his or her mind elsewhere? If you obviously can't hold your prospect's attention, perhaps you need to ask more questions. You may be telling or talking too much. Remember, a statement is worth about half as much as a question.

When the prospect says something, what is he or she looking at? If the prospect tells you, "Now isn't a great time for me," but while the words come out he or she is staring right at the product, you need to really be hearing him or her say, "Boy, would I love to own that." In another scenario, is the person furtively looking at his or her watch or at the clock? Perhaps you need to speed things up. If you take your sweet time, this prospect may leave before you even get to the finale. Consolidate your presentation, highlight the important parts, and then get to the point. A busy prospect (and most people are busy) will appreciate this adjustment you made for him or her.

The heart and soul of any presentation involves building value and creating need. Experienced salespeople do this while weaving a web of mini-closes, asking questions, listening, and responding with tie downs. Selling with finesse, asking rather than telling, and helping prospects feel as if they are arriving at a decision instead of being forced to accept your point of view is more effective than attempting to overpower them.

Make sure you don't mistake this approach for weakness of any sort. *In fact, this is the most powerful approach in all of selling!* After making a sale, your goal is not to hear your prospect say, "Whew, you're a good salesperson!" Your goal needs to be to hear him or her say, "I've been thinking I needed something just like this before you came by!" You can then leave your presentation happy, knowing you're on your way to becoming a millionaire.

Chapter Fifteen

———— $ ————

The Presentation—
The Four-Step Process to Success

"What's your goal during a presentation? In a nutshell, you want to build value, create need, and get the prospect to agree with your point of view."
Brian Gotta

What can make a great presentation? There are several more facets to making a great presentation. When you can develop a system for doing a presentation that is cohesive, comprehensive, and easily duplicated, you'll be able to zero in on your selling points more effectively and more quickly than if you endeavor to "wing it" each time. Make everything as simple as possible in its execution, while complex and subtle in its effectiveness. Following is a simple, clear and easy to master outline for putting on a great presentation. It contains four steps that are the core of an effective call.

View Yourself Objectively

While you're doing a presentation, picture yourself as your prospect sees you. Everything you've read about enthusiasm, eagerness, and friendliness amounts to nothing if you're not sincere and professional. Pretend you have a videotape of yourself during a sales presentation and critique yourself. Are you engaging while not being overly or falsely friendly? Are you making eye contact and speaking up with confidence, instead of looking away and mumbling?

How are you handling objections within the presentation? Do you visibly let them bother you? Do you get defensive and argumentative? Or do you accept them as valid points while you offer a strong counterpoint?

Most of all, are you friendly, enthusiastic, and at least mildly entertaining? If you're not, you can be. If you prefer not to work on yourself and your charm, however, you won't have much fun, which means the prospect won't have much fun, which means you won't get the *opportunity* to close a sale very often.

The Four-Step Presentation Outline

All products and services, tangible or intangible, share some basic similarities in how they are sold. Though you'll adapt the following to your particular situation, the simplicity and clarity of what they accomplish make the steps useful no matter what you are offering.

What's your goal during a presentation? In a nutshell, you want to build value, create need, and get the prospect to agree with your point of view. All of the techniques you've learned so far are vehicles designed so you can accomplish one goal: To build enough value and create enough need that you have an opportunity to close. There are four basic steps to accomplishing this task:

1. *Show a feature*. Every product and service has a list of features and benefits. Use them as your way of distinguishing your product and yourself from the competition. The more of these you show, the better chance you have to sell. When you *show a feature,* you need to do so with excitement. This doesn't have to mean you're giddy with joy over a price sheet, statistic or a warranty. But when you convey a real sense of pleasure about what you offer, it comes across as sturdy belief in what you're presenting.

2. *Elicit a positive response.* After showing a feature, ask the prospect to agree with you that it is a benefit. A question designed to get a favorable response such as *"Isn't that nice?"* is important. This step will help you determine if the prospect understands everything you're saying. More importantly, it almost always gains you a yes response from the prospect.

This doesn't mean you need to stop what you're doing after this question and demand an answer. However, dropping in an "Isn't that nice?"—almost as if you and the prospect are *both* discovering the product *together* for the first time— makes your offering more appealing. The real importance of this step is a cumulative one. When you list twenty features, each followed by the prospect nodding and saying yes, there's a good chance the prospect will say it again when you ask for the sale.

3. *Reiterate the need.* By telling the prospect that he or she needs your product or service, you're planting a seed. Remind yourself that *you* are the expert in your field, not the prospect. If you went to a mechanic today because you heard a squeaking noise every time you slowed down and he or she looked under the car and said, "Looks like you need new brakes," what would you likely do? Chances are you'd get new brakes.

Likewise, if you went to a doctor for an ailment, and the doctor said to take a prescription for two weeks, are you going to tell your doctor, "I don't think I need it"? Of course not. Since your doctor has earned your trust, you know he or she won't misguide you. As a result, you're going to do as the doctor tells you.

Sales is no different. Like the doctor or mechanic, you are the expert. As long as you act ethically and morally, you're the one who best knows what the prospect *needs*. Yet often in sales, the salesperson lacks the confidence to simply look a prospect in the eye and say the same thing the mechanic or the doctor says, "You need it."

4. *Transition to step one.* What you're presenting possibly has more than just one feature. Therefore you'll need to transition back to step one to tell your prospect about the next feature. You can accomplish this easily by telling him or her you need to show or explain something else.

Here are the four steps put into action twice:

1. **You show your prospect a feature.**
2. **You:** "Isn't that nice?"
   Prospect: "That's great."
3. **You:** "You really need something like this."
4. **You:** "Now let me show you this real quick."
5. **You show the prospect another feature.**
6. **You:** "Isn't that great?"
   Prospect: "Very nice."
7. **You:** "That's something you really seem to need too."
8. **You:** "And take a look at this real quick."

In a rudimentary sense, this is really all you need to do a successful presentation. Of course there will be much more involved when you actually get in front of the person. You'll use tie down phrases and "if...then" questions. You'll compliment the prospect, handle any objections, give out a high price to raise his or her expectations, and many other components you will learn through experience.

The primary task you have is to build the value of what you are offering and get the prospect to acknowledge a need for it. That's it. Then all you need to do is close the sale.

Feel Free to Say It Again

You may have noticed in the above exercise that some of the same statements were repeated. There's a reason for this, which is Law Number Six: *The prospect only hears a percentage of what you say*. If you have some convincing points you want to get across, you may have to mention them more than once before they sink in.

As a result, learning ways to say the same thing with different phrasing becomes an invaluable skill. Going back to the four steps again, let's look at numbers two, three and four.

After showing a feature, you'll slip in "Isn't that nice?" and almost always get an affirmative response from the prospect. Other phrases like "Isn't that great?" or "Won't that be easy?" or "Would you use that if you had it?" get the same response without you sounding like a broken record. But don't worry if you do repeat phrases often. Your prospect is concentrating on your product or service, not on the quantity of identical sentences you have used.

After you've shown a feature and asked "Isn't that nice?" (to which the prospect replied "yes"), you need to place in a statement of need. The most direct way is saying, "This is something you need." However, that statement is strong and perhaps needs to be used later after you build more value.

Coming on a little less strongly but with the same effect would be a phrase such as:

"It seems like this would really make things easier for you."
"This feature would really give you peace of mind."
"It seems like you need this."
"In your situation this feature is really important."

The key is to establish your wording. You're not just showing your prospect something nice, fancy and extravagant. You're showing something your prospect *needs*. Just saying it once is not enough. The more your prospect hears it, the more he or she believes it.

The final phrase in the process, "Now let me show this real quick," is just a simple transition. Unless you're in a unique situation where he or she isn't pressed for time, you need to imply that you're moving along and keeping his or her time restraints in mind.

The more times you say the words "real quick" in the presentation, the more the presentation will give the prospect the feeling that it's moving along. How? Real quickly. No sooner than those words leave your lips, you're dynamically and confidently back to showing another feature, building more value, creating more need, and gaining affirmation.

The Four-Step Presentation in Action

When put together in sequence, the four-step process will make any presentation more compelling and efficient. Consider the product or service you want to market. What are the essential facts and features that make it attractive? List ten or twenty of them and label them starting with "Feature One" and so on down the list. When presenting these features, your description will sound similar to this:

"(Explain Feature One)—isn't that nice? That seems to be something you could really use. Now let me show you this real quick. (Explain Feature Two)—that's great isn't it? You really do need something like this. Now I'll show you this quickly. (Explain Feature Three)—won't that be fantastic to have? Now real quick take a look at this. (Explain Feature Four)—isn't that fantastic? It's something that's really going to pay off. That's why you need to have it." And continue on for each feature you want to explain.

Simply reading what is above makes the process seem elementary and repetitious. Remember, however, that each feature will take anywhere from thirty seconds to several minutes to properly explain. By the time you have segued into "Isn't that nice? You really need it" and "Let me show you this real quick," the prospect is not even aware of the repetition involved. He or she is more concerned with your product's or service's value, price and need.

Selling anything is a detailed process. However, with a basic format or outline to follow, you'll never get lost or flustered during your presentation because you'll always have a touchstone to refer to. It will be clear to your prospects exactly what you want to accomplish and what they will gain by doing business with you. By following this simple structure and adding your own personal touches, you can look like a pro to any prospect. They're likely to see you as a sales veteran and a millionaire in the making.

Chapter Sixteen

— $ —

Now Is the Time!

*"If you weren't dedicated before,
you can become dedicated now. If you haven't had
an opportunity before, you have one now."*
Brian Gotta

What do you *really* want out of life? Maybe you would like a nicer home and cars, college education for your children, the ability to travel more, a very comfortable retirement, and no money challenges? Look at the people who have those things and more. You'll soon realize they not only have all of the above, but also one other very important thing: freedom. They have the freedom to make more choices and be more in control of their lives.

So What Does It Take to Be *Free?*

Nearly everyone living the financial good life has several things in common. First, they all decided there was no reason they couldn't earn a lot of money, and so they developed a plan to do so. That plan contained an element of risk, but all of these successful people knew they had the ability to bounce back from adversity, to get up, dust themselves off, and keep going.

Most importantly, the majority of people who we would classify as being financially successful are extremely disciplined. They invested a lot of very hard and smart work to get where they are. No one handed anything to them, and they didn't feel anything was owed to them because of who they were, what college they attended, or what their previous experiences were. All they wanted was an opportunity and the promise of being rewarded for their hard work. Does any of this sound like you?

In sales you are paid by results, not the number of hours spent. You're paid more for effort than for talent. A sales career or business, with a disciplined, goal-oriented, never-say-die attitude, can only mean one thing: wealth and prosperity *to you!*

Go Out and Get It Before It's Too Late

If you haven't already done so, make up your mind right now that yours will not be a life of mediocrity. If anyone can succeed, you certainly can. You now have plenty of tools to help you be successful in your sales career or business. However, just reading and dreaming about it isn't enough. The sweetest and grandest of dreams mean nothing until you *do* something. Just *saying* you'll do something isn't good enough. Remember Ben Franklin's advice: "Well done is better than well said." Apply his words to what you've learned and you can become "Healthy, wealthy and wise."

There's No Time Like the Present

Jonathan was once a highly regarded high school basketball star. He was recruited by more than one of the major universities and went to the school of his choice. His promise for the future was unlimited, and so was his potential. Four years later he spent his senior year on the bench, watching younger students play for the team he'd been expected to star on.

"When I came out of high school I had it all," Jonathan explains. "Between the scholarships, press clippings, and all-star games, I thought I was *it*. The problem was I had it *too* easy. When I showed up for practice at the university I wasn't used to working too hard and didn't think I needed to. The coach kept telling me that things were different in college, that this wasn't high school anymore.

"Since I didn't believe him, I took it easy on sprints and didn't push myself in the weight room. I regarded college as just a stopover on my way to the next level. Even though most of the guys were better than I was—bigger, stronger, and faster—I didn't buckle down. I figured all freshmen go through an adjustment period and it would all come naturally.

"Well, it didn't come naturally. I kept procrastinating throughout my sophomore and junior years. I kept thinking, 'Next practice I'm going to break out and show them what I can do,' but I still had the same bad habits. I thought about transferring for a while because I blamed the coach, but I liked my teammates and the school. Deep down inside I knew it wasn't anybody's fault but mine that I wasn't playing.

"Finally, my senior year came and I made a resolution to work harder, and I did. I gave it a hundred percent in practice and had some of the old juice come back. By then, though, we had a team of younger players who already passed me by. I was one step slower than them, and they were that much stronger. The coach trusted them in the game more than me. By the end of the year, I was only getting in when we had a big lead or were getting beat.

"I'll never forget my last game of the season. I figured that since I was a senior I'd play a lot, but it didn't work out that way. The game was close, and if we wanted to go to the postseason tournament, we had to win. The coach kept looking at me, and I kept looking at him, but he kept passing me up. He actually seemed sad when he looked at me.

"In the end, we didn't win. When there were just two minutes left on the clock, it finally hit me: 'This is *it*. It's *over*.' When we went down by seven with 30 seconds left, the coach called me. I went in. Since it was an away game and no one in the stands knew me, nobody clapped or even noticed I went in except my teammates. They all patted me on the back and told me to 'go for it.' That thirty seconds seemed like one second. The buzzer went off and that was it. My career was over.

"I know now I blew it. There's no one to blame but me. If I'd worked as hard as the other guys on the team, it may have ended differently. If I had been better, maybe the team would have been better. If I could go back and start over knowing what I know now, it would be a different story. But now it's too late."

Get Started Today

Whether you're a freshman, sophomore, junior, or senior in your career or business, now is the time to make a comeback. If you weren't dedicated before, you can become dedicated now. If you haven't had an opportunity before, you have one now.

Someday, sooner than you might think, your last game is going to be here. When you've taken that jersey off for the last time and your career or business activities are over, how do you want to look back on what you've accomplished? How do you want your teammates and your family to see you? Are you going to be the one who "never got a break," or are you going to be in control and make your dreams come true?

Form excellent daily habits. Set daily, weekly, monthly, annual, and five-year career or business goals. Reward yourself often after accomplishing your goals. See to it that no matter what happens, nothing causes you to swerve off your course. And though you may at times get discouraged, don't ever give up—just keep on going.

The time will come when you'll have climbed that mountain of prosperity. You'll look down below at all the others who weren't willing to pay the price you paid to get there. They'll all wish they were where you are, but they're still waiting for a free ride to the top. And as they get older and realize that no one is ever going to give them a free ride and that now it's too late to start climbing, you'll look in their eyes and see regret.

But rest assured that their regret will never be a part of you. You woke up from your dream, got out of bed, and went to work. *Congratulations! You're a millionaire!*

About the Author

Brian Gotta graduated from Indiana University with a BA in English Literature. He began his sales career selling high-end vacuum cleaners "door to door." He worked his way into senior management with a large international direct sales company, eventually overseeing all recruiting and growth projects at its home office. Brian has a keen acumen for sales, sales management, and recruiting, having built one of the largest teams of direct sales professionals on the West Coast.

Brian is an expert teacher, trainer, and motivational speaker who has helped thousands of individuals maximize their potential and achieve their dreams. He is also a committed husband and father of four children, and coaches several youth sports leagues.

Brian can be reached via his website at www.booksbygotta.com or e-mail at brian@booksbygotta.com.

THE MAN WHO THINKS HE CAN

If you think you are beaten, you are;
If you think you dare not, you don't;
If you'd like to win, but think you can't,
It's almost a cinch you won't.
If you think you'll lose, you're lost,
For out in the world we find
Success begins with a fellow's will;
It's all in the state of mind.

If you think you're outclassed, you are;
You've got to think high to rise.
You've got to be sure of yourself before
You can ever win a prize.
Life's battles don't always go
To the stronger or faster man;
But soon or late the man who wins
Is the man who thinks he can.

Walter D. Wintle

Other Books by *Possibility Press*

No Excuse!...Key Principles for Balancing Life and Achieving Success
No Excuse! I'm Doing It...How to Do Whatever It Takes to Make It Happen
No Excuse! The Workbook...Your Companion to the Book to
Help You Live the "No Excuse!" Lifestyle
Reject Me—I Love It!...21 Secrets for Turning Rejection Into Direction
If They Say No, Just Say NEXT!...24 Secrets for Going Through
the Noes to Get to the Yeses
The Electronic Dream...Essential Ingredients for Growing a
People Business in an e-Commerce World
Time And Money.com...Create Wealth by Profiting from
the Explosive Growth of E-Commerce
Are You Living Your Dream?...How to Create Wealth and
Live the Life You Want...You Can Do It!
If It Is To Be, It's Up To Me...How to Develop the Attitude of a
Winner *and* Become a Leader
Get A GRIP On Your Dream...12 Ways to Squeeze More Success Out of Your Goals
Are You Fired Up?...How to Ignite Your Enthusiasm and
Make Your Dreams Come True
Dream Achievers...50 Powerful Stories of People Just Like You
Who Became Leaders in Network Marketing
Full Speed Ahead...Be Driven by Your Dream to Maximize
Your Success and Live the Life You Want
Focus On Your Dream...How to Turn Your Dreams and Goals Into Reality
SOAR To The Top...Rise Above the Crowd and Fly Away to Your Dream
In Business And In Love...How Couples Can Successfully
Run a Marriage-Based Business
Schmooze 'Em Or Lose 'Em...How to Build High-Touch
Relationships in a High-Tech World
SCORE Your Way To Success...How to Get Your Life on Target
What Choice Do I Have?...How to Make Great Decisions for Tremendous Outcomes
Dump The Debt And Get Free...A Realistic and Sensible Plan to
Eliminate Debt and Build Wealth in the 21st Century
Brighten Your Day With Self-Esteem...How to Empower, Energize
and Motivate Yourself to a Richer, Fuller, More Rewarding Life
Naked People Won't Help You...Keep Your Cool, Capture the
Confidence, and Conquer the Fear of Public Speaking

Tapes by *Possibility Press*

Turning Rejection Into Direction...A Roundtable Discussion With
Network Marketing Independent Business Owners

Notes

Notes